COMMUNICATION MEDIA AND SOCIAL CHANGES

COMMUNICATION MEDIA AND SOCIAL CHANGES

Editor

Prof. Ramesh Chandra

ISHA BOOKS

DELHI-110 033

Communication Media and Social Changes

Rs. 750

ISBN: 81-8205-066-9

Published in 2008 in India by
Isha Books, D-43, Prithviraj Road,
Adarsh Nagar, Delhi-110 033

Laser Typesetting at : Shree Vaishnavi Creations, Delhi
Printed at : Vishal Kaushik Printers Delhi

Contents

Preface *vii*

1. **Media: The New Communicator** 1
Media Relations.

2. **Participatory Communication** 24
Radio; Video; Theatre; The Internet; Challenges of Participatory Communication; Community Multimedia Centres.

3. **Media and Social Changes** 88
Social Change Media; Current Trends in Communications Environment; Communication Strategies to Control HIV/AIDS; Media and Social Change in Arabic World.

4. **Media and Gender Development** 140
Media's Approches to Gender Development; Media's Stand on Violence Against Women.

5. **Media and Violence** 200
Media's Influence on Children; Role of Communication in Preventing Crime.

6. **Strategies of Developmental Communication** 214
Dominant Paradigm in the Field of Development Communication; Theoretical Convergence;

Emerging Trends in Communciation Development.

Bibliography 293

Index 295

Preface

Communication for social change is part of an evolution of communications methodology that can help accelerate global development. The process began in the first quarter of the 20th century with the use of publicity tools to bring attention to social problems such as hunger and disease. It grew to a reliance on public relations as a means of identifying stakeholders and creating programs to fit the audience's interests.

Media can play a much greater role in enabling people to take control over their own lives, in enabling people and societies to set their own agendas in relation to political, economic and social development; and in enabling, in particular, the voices of the economically and politically marginalised to be amplified and channelled to mainstream public and political debate.

The use of electronic media for social change has already seen an impressive evolution. Since the fifties many associations, unions, community groups or NGOs, have challenged the dominant radio and television networks with small stations broadcasting towards specific communities. While bigger and bigger trusts are concentrating the control of the most influential mass media in the world, alternative networks of information and communication are flourishing often supported by the use of Internet.

The new communication technologies have the capacity to navigate from one media to another, to choose between the multiple communication tools and adapt strategies to a particular situation. They have recently opened enormous possibilities in terms of the horizontal cultural exchanges that communities and individuals can develop across the world. The meaning of community may broaden to groups that have common interests though from different cultures. Access is gradually being granted by social groups and individuals that were previously marginalised.

This book elaborately discusses the role and impact of communication media in social change. It will serve as a highly informative reference tool for all concerned.

Editor

1

Media: The New Communicator

Whatever we plan for the future in terms of social change should associate in one strategy the objective of social change, the knowledge of new technologies and the process of communication. None of these alone can achieve, and the three together can't either if the human factor is not in the essence of the reflection: the new communicator should be the center-piece of the communication strategies for social change in the next century.

The more we invest in development, more we contribute to the growing of the cemetery of development, the striking vision of dust over computers that only worked a few months, water pumps that lasted one or two years only, huge construction machines on the side of roads that were never completed. We have seen in a small town of Burkina Faso a brand new construction for a hospital which never opened its doors because there were no nurses and doctors to run it. We have seen two thousand post office mail boxes rusting under the rain in a village of five hundred illiterate families who neither received or wrote letters. We have seen water being wasted during months from a tap at a very dry village in the south Saharan belt known as Sahel, because nobody would spend about 3 US$ dollars to buy a part to repair the faucet. W have seen expensive and sophisticated OB vans (mobile television studios) grounded for years because their tires were flat. In Nigeria, UNICEF donated to the government more than one thousand 4 x 4 jeeps and pick-ups during the immunisation campaigns of 1988-1990, few are still on the road. The backyard of the Ministry of Education in Haiti looks like a cemetery of automobiles; brand new jeeps donated by the international cooperation agencies are piled after being virtually destroyed by accidents or due to the absolute lack of maintenance.

Anyone who has experience working with international developing agencies or NGOs, knows that these things happen every day and that we are often obliged to close our eyes in order to avoid "conflict" with government partners. Corruption is obviously part of it and the international developing system, call it United Nations, USAID, or any other name, has been somehow hiding the implications that it has for social development.

Almost everybody now—from the smallest community based NGO to the development gurus at the World Bank in Washington— seem to agree that projects fail because the community is not involved. The nature of projects was decided without any form of dialogue with the community of so called "beneficiaries". Vertical projects are not sensitive to social and cultural aspects of reality. If participation is not encouraged, communities are passive about development projects that are supposed to improve their living conditions. Communities do not have the sense of ownership of projects that were decided and implemented with a top-down approach. A water system was installed by technicians from the government agency with support from an international development organisation. Who owns the project? We have at least three different scenarios:

a) the project never involved anybody from the community

b) community was only invited to "contribute" with labor, or

c) once the project is almost completed, community is invited to "organise" and take over.

It is onvious that from these three scenarios we are likely to expect a non-sustainable project. The community is at the most challenged with a new responsibility, with no preparation for it. When the first hand pump breaks down, people just wait until somebody from the government shows up to repair it. Community participation can not "fix" the problem afterwards, it should be a component as important as the funding and it should be developed along with the funding process. No funds, no project in the short term. No participation, no project in the long run. Actually, participation is the way how the community funds the project. Every body seems to know this. Any publication by UN agencies or bilateral development agencies will state the importance of community participation and community ownership of projects. How many of these agencies translate what is written on paper to an actual process at the community level? Most of them simply don't know how to do it.

Community participation may be the hottest trend in development but is mostly words, not facts. It may even be part of the World Bank's or UNDP policy in development countries, but there is no mechanism to guarantee it will happen. To start, few agencies have at the field level people that have certain knowledge and experience in community participation. Most of them just improvise by adding the participation and communication tasks to the job description of any professional, regardless of his or her academic background and experience. Often, the responsibility is given to experts who spend most of their time flying from one continent to another, attending important programme meetings, reading and drafting sharp documents with recommendations, but have little or no experience of working at the community level. They miss the whole cultural dimension of development.

A quick look at the profile of field staff in most developing organisations shows that if there is anyone in charge of the "participation" aspect, this is usually someone of a lower professional level. That is why many of these organisations often rely on NGOs for the "participatory" approach. But even within the NGO world, what is the profile of an "expert" in participation? How are the specialists recruited? Which is their background? A professional from the social sciences, education, anthropology or sociology might be in a better position to understand participation than an economist or an engineer. At a few international agencies, like UNICEF or FAO, communicators are in charge of the community participation component. This is, at least, an acknowledgment of the role of communication in development.

In the early nineties, UNICEF realised that its information and communications officers at the field level were appointed under about 50 different names. From the straight forward "communication" or "information" officer, to "social mobilisation", "advocacy", "development support communication", "community mobilisation", "social marketing", "development communication", "media", "external relations", "public relations" officers. Even the distinction between "communication" and "information" is not very clear to many. As it is true that the word "communication" is a wider concept that contains all the others, it is also important to make the difference between the one-way (information) and the two-way (communication) process. It helps at least to distinguish the journalists from the communicators.

Journalist are often labeled as experts in communication. There is little knowledge about how the communication work covers a very wide range of skills that a journalist is not prepared to deal with. A journalist is prepared to work with the media, to write, to report, to produce for radio, television and newspapers. By appointing journalists to posts that are designed for specialists in communication, agencies are already doing a choice to work mostly towards mass media. Nonetheless, there is little choice. There are thousands of journalists but very few specialists in communication. The schools of journalism can be counted by hundreds in the whole world, each one producing every year dosens of journalists or public relations professionals. On the other hand, there are no schools to train communication professionals. Many universities decided to change the name to their school of journalism, but the contents remains almost the same in the apparently new "schools of social communication". Information has been too easily merged with communication. Actually, it might be important to remember that from its etymological origin communication is participation.

A new communicator is usually someone who owes at least 50% of his or her qualification to a wide range of experiences that have little to do with his or her own academic background. What actually makes the "new communicator" is this mixture of experience in development, a special sensibility to work with communities, and the knowledge of communication tools and technologies. A new communicator has to balance a very practical approach to social reality, with the capacity to elaborate and conceptualise strategies. The academic background is somehow irrelevant, given the fact that there are no institutions that provide specific training of this type. Educators, anthropologists, agronomists often make good communicators when they add to their field experience on development and community participation the knowledge of the communication process and the skills to handle information technologies. Journalists already have this knowledge, though limited to the media, but they can also become new communicators -enriched with a holistic vision of communication- if exposed to the experience of development and community work.

This is not to say that only inter-personal communication is needed in the context of social change. The community based approach is often a result of the total lack of access to the information channels. It can be the only possible strategy given the extreme process of marginalisation that some communities may suffer. Nonetheless, the new technologies have recently opened enormous possibilities in terms of the horizontal cultural exchanges that communities and individuals can develop across the world. The meaning of community may broaden to groups that have common interests though from different cultures. Access is gradually being granted by social groups and individuals that were previously marginalised.

The use of electronic media for social change has already seen an impressive evolution. Since the fifties many associations, unions, community groups or NGOs, have challenged the dominant radio and television networks with small stations broadcasting towards specific communities. While bigger and bigger trusts are concentrating the control of the most influential mass media in the world, alternative networks of information and communication are flourishing often supported by the use of Internet.

The challenges of communication are constantly evolving, as new possibilities but also new needs emerge. The new communicator has the capacity to navigate from one media to another, to choose between the multiple communication tools and adapt strategies to a particular situation. His or her experience may range from helping to strengthen union organisations to covering social issues for media stations, devising participation strategies for development projects at the community level, facilitating the networking of non-governmental organisations, and/ or producing educational materials. This flexibility to use communication strategies in various cultural contexts provides a training that is second to none.

The following could be the main premises for the new communicator:

— The new communicator must be equipped with the understanding that technology is a tool and nothing else but a tool. Technology may support the communication process, but the latter should not be totally dependent on it. Also, it is important to understand that technology doesn't only involve computers, satellites and Internet. A pencil is an astonishing piece of technology, and communication techniques that have proved their efficacity range from popular theater to community murals.

— The new communicator must deeply understand that communication for social change deals essentially with culture and a very special sensitivity is needed to support the process of social change in a developing world that has nothing else to hold on to than its cultural identity. Development and social change must be possible within a process of horizontal and respectful cultural exchanges.

— The new communicator must be familiar with this concept: in communication for social change the process is more important than the products. In journalism, the articles, the video documentaries, or the radio programmes are valuable results for a skilled professional. But in social change and development, the process of communication with the people and within the communities is more important than the printed or audio-visual aids that may emerge from that dynamic. Is in the process of communication and participation that social change starts to happen.

Media Relations

Public information, public relations, communication: international institutions seem to use these words interchangeably, moving from one to another and back again as successive waves of 'reform' come and go. Are they different from one another? And are they complementary or contradictory?

In publicly financed institutions such as UNESCO, public information constitutes an organic function. Keeping the public abreast of developments and debates in the worlds of education, science, culture, social sciences and communication is one of the reasons for which UNESCO exists. Doing it and doing it right is not only clever; it is an essential part of UNESCO's mandate. Reflecting UNESCO's broad and diverse areas of responsibility, its Bureau of Public Information seeks to draw attention to a wide range of activities. In doing so, it relies on the research and expertise of colleagues throughout the house to spotlight important social and ethical issues, to nurture the democratic debate – with facts, figures and analysis – and to press for change where change is required. Public information is, in other words, one of the organization's principal weapons in the pursuit of its fundamental objectives.

There is enormous, probably limitless interest in the public and media for new data and insights on issues that are UNESCO's bread and butter, such as cloning and bioethics in general, the state of oceans and coastlines, the sharing of freshwater resources, the education of girls, the digital divide, freedom of the press, teachers' salaries and working conditions, endangered cultural treasures – the list is a long one. This demand affords UNESCO with constantly renewed opportunities to advertise its concerns and programmes to irrigate public opinion with its values. In all cases however, what the public and media hunger for is information about the issue itself, not about the institution – and even less about its servants or component units. Failing to recognize this as self-evident is a recipe failure.

Results periodically achieved – massive, worldwide media coverage of UNESCO's reports and initiatives on EFA, trafficking of cultural goods, underwater heritage, disappearing languages, for example – have underlined the enormous appeal of the research and analysis for which UNESCO is uniquely qualified. More, better and more frequent reports are needed to meet that demand – and put UNESCO back in the news.

Addressing as it must, complex, often painful social realities, public information that emanates from United Nations agencies cannot please all of the people all of the time. Genuine information is, by definition, a challenge to complacency which may at times lead to controversy and elicit protests. Seeking at all costs to avoid such developments is incompatible with the public information function. While there can be no place for gratuitous provocation, it must be accepted that no one has ever produced an omelette – in this case achieving influence over public opinion – without breaking some eggs. Public information's essential currency is credibility in the eyes of the media. International organizations know, by painful experience, that this is not a given. Achieving and maintaining media credibility is above all an exercise in transparency which should be undertaken on the understanding that the reputation of international organizations must and will ultimately rest on the quality and relevance of their 'real world' contribution.

In the private sector as in politics, public relations are more often than not a question of putting one's best foot forward. Success is never guaranteed. Businesses and politicians are expected to have public relation strategies, but to describe their pronouncements as 'PR' is not a compliment. In plain English it means rubbish, or something ruder. Taxpayer-financed institutions cannot afford risks of this kind. They look especially bad when suspected of selfpromotion or empty posturing.

Public relations for organizations like UNESCO should mean one thing only: exchanging information and developing working relations with different target audiences – constituents, parliamentarians, international organizations, provincial and municipal authorities, civic groups, NGOs, academic institutions, religious organizations, private enterprises – using language and supports appropriate to each. Public relations are, first and foremost, about dialogue. Their purpose is to build networks, to forge temporary or lasting alliances in order to achieve programme objectives: ratifications, project completions, policy changes, for example. In some instances this dialogue should lead to operational partnerships, fund raising and other forms of collaboration. Public relations thereby represent an important entry point into the UN system for a wide range of potential partners.

It stands to reason therefore that responsibility for engaging in public relations cannot be left to any single department. They must be conducted, as a matter of course and on a permanent basis, by directors and programme managers, indeed by all substantive officers at Headquarters and in the field. Some will, on occasion, require material support. All rightfully expect policy guidance. Information kits and videos are welcome but not nearly as important as a regular internal flow of information on what must be clear, coherent and vigorously pursued objectives.

Communication

What is left to 'communication' is the heart of the matter, that which speaks louder than words: action. What will always matter more than what we say is what we do – or fail to do. Communications suffuse every aspect of the work of most UN bodies and agencies, including UNESCO. Standards, guidelines, codes of conduct, technical assistance: all are about sharing and spreading knowledge and values in order to affect change.

Successful communications imply transparency – public information – and outreach – public relations. But they, above all, require courage, conviction and initiative. Valuebased endeavours are judged in the end, not by the noise they temporarily generate but by the difference they make in the lives of people. Nothing new there. What is perhaps new in a number of international organizations is a growing reliance on marketing techniques long on image-polishing but short on substance: glitter-studded media-oriented events, contrived 'photo opportunities', glossy brochures. Some also seem more comfortable with slogans and sound bites, with ghostwritten 'op-ed' pieces on consensual subjects than with the rougher give and take of press conferences and interviews with well-informed, aggressive reporters. Those who claim expertise and leadership in social, economic or humanitarian matters, among others, must expect searching questions. These are inherent to democratic processes and should be welcomed as management tools.

There is nothing wrong with gloss and glitter or with controlled appearances in the media provided these come in addition to – and not as a substitute for – genuine public information and public relations activities. One comes down to what you can afford. The other reflects – and projects – how significant you might be.

Public Information

A -classic mistake is to think of Public Information as a support service, on a par with personnel or procurement. The truth is that keeping the public informed and alive to issues under the organization's mandate is a core function: one of the reasons why the organization exists. Its purpose is to: share knowledge/ raise awareness/change attitudes / mobilize support/change policies. Public information should not be confused with advertising or propaganda, though these may be by-products. The image and reputation of international organizations depends less on self-proclaimed successes than on the relevance and quality of their real-world contributions. Institutions of the United Nations system must set their own media agenda. It is amazing how many senior UN officers turn to PI professionals for assistance only when facing hostile questions from media. It is almost always too late by then. Experience suggests that persistent criticism, when it occurs, is, in most cases, richly deserved. Better to have been in the media regularly, with stories based on the organization's own analysis and activities, so that criticism, when it comes, can be put into perspective.

International organizations must communicate with multiple audiences: Governments, other international organizations, NGOs, academic institutions, parliamentarians, local authorities, professional networks, schools, the public at large. All deserve attention, but it is rarely possible to communicate successfully with all at once.

Different tools are required to communicate with different audiences:

- *Governments, IGOs*: meetings and documents.
- *NGOs, networks of specialists*: web, newsletters.
- *Schools*: teaching aids, kits, posters.
- *Constituency* (National commissions, partners, staff): magazine.

- *Parliamentarians*: hearings, brochures, tailored briefings.
- *Media*: press releases, B-rolls, press conferences, media advisories.

It is counterproductive to issue a press release containing no real information for the sole purpose of pleasing a partner or donor. Doing so regularly, as so many organizations do, does great harm to credibility and makes it difficult to be taken seriously by the media.

Story-telling

To capture the media's – and the public's – attention, you must have a story to tell. And you must remember that a story is always based on substance – the real lives of real people – almost never on institutional process. Meetings, conferences, round-tables do not by themselves constitute stories. What the public and the media hunger for is information about the issues those events are supposed to address, not about the inner workings of institutions. Failing to recognize this as self-evident is a common mistake – and a recipe for failure. Stories are almost always about people. Refugees, victims of war or epidemics, girls in school, citizens with access to the internet: are their numbers rising/declining? Is their situation improving/worsening? Where? Since when? According to whom? Who is doing what about it? What are the prospects/obstacles?

The really successful stories – those picked up by all, or nearly all, major media in a given country or region – are almost always based on solid, up-to-date reports providing analysis and comparative statistics.

A news-oriented approach

All media play a role in shaping public opinion, but none are more important than the mass media: morning newspapers, evening news programmes on television and news bulletins on radio all day long. To reach out to them it makes sense to adopt a news-oriented approach. News = story + today. It's as simple as that. While process (meetings, conferences, seminars) almost never constitutes a story in itself, it often does provide the required hook. Hook = the event you hang the story on to turn it into news. Examples: An issue to be addressed at a meeting opening... TOMORROW / An appeal made in a speech delivered... TODAY.

Identify stories of potential interest and the hook allowing you, on a given day, to turn it into news. The resulting calendar of media-oriented activities = a Media Action Plan. Analytical reports (on literacy rates, the number of girls in school, the state of coastlines, the distribution of water resources, etc.) provide some of the best opportunities to attract media interest. Those providing quantified and comparative information are almost irresistible. Each should be the subject, at minimum, of a press release.

When a conference or meeting provides the hook, experience shows the best chance to attract the media's attention comes on the eve of the event when the story can focus on the issue and the stakes involved. A 'curtainraiser' spelling these out is more likely to be attractive than a press release based on the inevitably consensual conclusions reached at the meeting's end. Op-Ed (Opinion and Editorial) articles can be an excellent way to convey a message. Words of advice:

- An Op-Ed piece should be relatively short: approximately 600 words.
- It must be signed.
- It must be focused and make a point, clearly.
- If distributed internationally, it should be sent to no more than one newspaper per county.
- Before sending it, identify the editor responsible for Op-Eds, and send your text to his/her personal attention, with a brief covering note.

Disseminating information to the media

It must be accepted that the media, not institutions, set the rules. The first and most important of these is that news cannot wait. You must be aware of the production schedule of the media you are approaching. If a story reaches the media too late in the day, its chances of appearing on the evening news or in the papers the following morning are poor. Obvious, but bureaucracies have great difficulties with this. Clearance procedures routinely take far more time than they should resulting far too often in missed deadlines.

Morning newspapers all over the world run roughly along the same schedule. Journalists gather for the daily editorial meeting around 9 a.m. They emerge from it one hour later and start working their 'beat'. By 3 or 4 p.m., they are under pressure to finalize their article(s) for the following day's edition. That means that your best chance to reach them usefully is between 10 a.m. and 3 or 4 p.m. at the latest. In other words, a journalist's day, as far as you are concerned, is only five or six hours long.

Nor does a journalist's week last seven days. Weekend editions are usually put together by separate, smaller, crews. Much of the material they contain is 'pre-cooked', prepared in advance, leaving less space for last minute news. Issuing a story on a Friday (or a Thursday in Muslim countries) – for the weekend papers – should, for that reason, be avoided whenever possible. If your story is essentially about finance and economics, do not aim for the Monday papers. Because there is no stockexchange on weekends, many papers feature only token Business sections on Mondays, sections where your story might have had the best chance to appear. Holding a press conference at 6 p.m. on a Friday – the time most conferences seem to end – is next to useless.

Press Conferences

Too many are called for the wrong reasons, at the wrong time. A press conference is an information tool, not some sort of glamorous event. Its object is to convey new and specific information to the media, not to offer a prestige-bestowing stage to VIPs. There should preferably be one speaker, two at the most, accompanied by a moderator whose role is to call the conference to order, give the floor to the main speaker, direct the question and answer period and call a close to the proceedings.

The main speaker may be accompanied by a small number of colleagues who should sit on the sidelines. But the majority of the people in the room should be journalists, not staff members and assorted personnel. The main speaker should keep his/her opening statement as short as the subject permits. 5 to 7 minutes is ideal. 20 minutes is almost certainly too much.

The best time for a press conference is between 11:00 a.m. and 2:30 p.m., weekdays. Calling a press conference in the evening, especially on the last working day of the week, is likely to have disappointing results. At the end of the press conference, time should be provided for brief one-on-one interviews with radio journalists and others.

Press Release

A press release detailing the information provided should be distributed to journalists attending the press conference and distributed widely, by fax or e-mail, to those who cannot. The goal is to get the information out, not to pack the room. The most important part of a press release is its opening paragraph. That is where the 'news' must be presented. If it is a survey/report you are presenting, tell us right away –in the very first sentence – what its main finding/conclusion is. And tell us immediately after that how significant that appears to be. If you are bringing attention to a meeting/conference, start by telling us what important issues it will be addressing, not by the formal title of the affair and the names of the presiding officers and VIPs in attendance.

Para 1 WHAT ('The number of girls entering secondary school/ the amount of freshwater available per capita/trafficking stolen art objects has risen/fallen over the past year/decade suggesting that ... according to UNESCO'). Para 2 WHO (UNESCO, in a study entitled '...'). WHEN (in a report made public Today/ in a conference opening Tomorrow).

WHERE (in Paris, New Delhi, Timbuktu...).

Para 3 This is a good place to include a quote, by the Director or the author of the report, for example, articulating the key message you want to convey. (If you make that quote up yourself, make sure the person quoted agrees...). Para 4 Develop para 1. How many girls, how much water Para 5 More on para 1.With what regional/ local variations? Highest/lowest figures.

Paras 6, 7, 8, maybe more Still more on para 1. *What, according* to the report, are the causes of these trends? There might be several, in which case a separate paragraph should be devoted to each significant one.

Final para(s) More on para 2. Place conference/report in wider context: is it part of a series? Are follow-up mechanisms/ meetings foreseen? Have similar surveys been conducted in other regions? This may be a good place to provide some web-links.

At the very end Give the name, phone number and e-mail of the person who can be contacted by journalists seeking more information.

Interviews

Interview requests are welcome. They should receive immediate attention. But that does not mean rushing in unprepared. If approached, find out first what the reporter is after and determine who in your office or beyond is best qualified to reply. The technical expert is often a better bet in this regard than the senior-most person available.

Anyone interviewed should stick to their areas of competence and responsibility and refuse to be drawn beyond these. Find out also what kind of media you are dealing with. If it is a newspaper you will want to know whether the story will be published in a specific section of the paper or in the news section. This will help you to picture the readers you are addressing. If it is radio, ask whether the interview will be live or recorded, and how long it will last. This will tell you how much you can hope to say.

Ask the reporter what areas he/she wishes to go into. In many countries, reporters will not agree to provide precise questions in advance, if only to avoid stilted answers. But most will readily discuss, in more general terms, the subject they are interested in. Give yourself the time to gather your thoughts. If the interview request comes by phone, ask the reporter to call back after 10 or 15 minutes, or call him/her back yourself. Do not over-rehearse your answers – it will only make you nervous – but force yourself to formulate beforehand the principal points you intend to make. Having done this, speak with the reporter promptly. Most are working on tight deadlines and may no longer be available if you wait too long.

In a radio or television interview you can only hope to make one, two or, at the very most, three distinct points. Make sure you have defined these in your head before starting the interview. Do not bring a crib sheet with a long list of points: you would likely choke on it. Right before the interview is about to start ask the reporter what his/her first question will be. This will help you to get off on the right foot. Once you have started, your initial – and perfectly natural – jitters will wear off.

Television

Feature length videos (25 minutes or more) are extremely expensive to produce and generally have a limited impact. Major television channels are rarely interested in institutional products of this kind and most, as a consequence, are watched by captive audiences only. It is much cheaper, and vastly more rewarding, to produce short (4–5 minutes), unedited videos – known as B-rolls in the trade – aimed at the evening news programmes watched by mass audiences.

B-rolls contain raw footage serving to illustrate the contents of a particular press release (floods/drought, teachers/ pupils/schools, cultural sites/events, etc.) thus making it attractive for television news programmes. B-rolls, by definition, do not contain voice-over commentaries. But they may, and should, include a brief (30 seconds) statement – a sound-bite - from an expert/ project manager/director articulating the key message being conveyed.

Each B-roll should be accompanied by a copy of the relevant press release and by a note – a 'dope sheet'– indicating precisely what is shown, for how many seconds and where it was shot B-rolls should be made available to television channels on magnetic tapes of the type used by professionals: Betacam (analogue or digital) or DV cam – not on the VHS tapes you may use at home. Make sure also to find out which system – Pal-SECAM or NTSC – is used by broadcasters in the country(ies) targeted for distribution.

Launching a major story: step by step

1 Fix an Embargo date and hour before which the story may not be published or broadcast and print it in bold lettering on all relevant material (report, executive summary, press release, B-roll) distributed to the media. Always give a GMT timeline if operating in more than one time zone. Do not make the mistake

of posting the press release on your website before the chosen hour: you would, by so doing, break your own embargo and make it impossible to ask discipline of others.

2 Two weeks or so before the embargo date, distribute a short media advisory – a 'teaser' – announcing the forthcoming release of a major report, promising answers to key questions raised (give examples). This will give editors time to prepare, order photos and graphs, ask for an editorial, dispatch reporters here and there to give a local flavour to the story, etc.

3 Write a detailed press release, including meaningful statistical tables whenever possible.

4 Make individual phone contacts with each of the media targeted and find within each one the person responsible for the department – Health, Education, Sciences, Culture, Business – most likely to be interested in your story. After doing it a few times, you will know whom to call. Beware of weekly magazines. Whereas daily newspapers are used to and tend to be respectful of embargos, weeklies are often tempted to ignore them if the release day does not suit them.

5 Hand carry or send by DHL/TNT/FedEx the press release, the report or document it is based on (on CD if too voluminous) and an Executive Summary of the report, if one is available, to each of the journalists who have confirmed interest.

6 Make experts available for interviews, under embargo, by phone or in person.

7 Contact the news department in all targeted television channels and offer the B-roll to them, taking time to

tell them what, in a nutshell, the story is about and what is on the B-roll.

8 Hold a press conference half an hour before the embargo is lifted.

9 Make experts available for radio interviews, in as many languages as possible, immediately following the press conference.

2

Participatory Communication

In Europe and the United States, the recent literature on communication for development often refers only to books and documents published in English. Studies on the theory of communication development will often include in their bibliography references to the same old paradigms: Lerner, Rogers, Schramm and some of the new ones: Jacobson, Servaes, White, Korten, Ascroft, Schiller or Habermas, among others.

The discussion on participatory communication has become popular since the 1980s, it is no less true that most of the existing experiences are still ignored. Much of the available literature is based on a handful of case stories, mostly drawn from countries where English is the enabling research tool. This is one of the reasons why the participatory communication experiences in Latin America which started in the late 1940s and now count in the thousands are taken into account far less by academics in Europe or North America.

While a much greater understanding of the role of communication in social change is now spread among development organisations, particularly in developing countries and among academics in industrialised countries, still, little is known about many concrete experiences and projects where communication has been or is instrumental in social change.

Because of the language barriers and the scarce international visibility of most of the grassroots experiences, there is much misunderstanding among development organisations, and even academic institutions, about the essence of participatory communication practices that are alive and well in developing nations. In spite of the increasing awareness about the relevance of participation in economic and social development, the concept of participatory communication still lacks an accurate definition that could contribute to a better understanding of the notion. But perhaps it's not so desperately needed.

Actually, participatory communication may not be defined easily because it cannot be considered a unified model of communication. The eagerness for labels and encapsulated definitions could only contribute to freeze a communication movement that is still shaping itself, and that may be more valuable precisely because of its variety and looseness.

The experiences of participatory communication for social change are as diverse as the cultural and geographic settings in which they have been developing.In spite of participatory communication being a relatively recent topic of interest for academics, its history spans over the last fifty years, from the time Radio Sutatenza started in a remote area of Colombia and the Bolivian miners organised to set up community radio stations in their mining districts. Latin America has generally been the nest where the first experiences originated. Nonetheless, with the end of authoritarian regimes in Africa and Asia during the past two decades, new experiences of participatory communication for social change have also blossomed in these regions.

The diversity of participatory communication experiences has always been a sign of its healthy status. However, the linkages with development projects aimed at economic and social change have not always been successful. It looks like, at the grassroots level, the need for communication has been deeply felt by the people who took action to make it possible, while at the planning and implementation level of donor and government driven projects there has been little consciousness about change.

The two ends are eventually going to meet, because of the international cooperation for development lessons learned during past decades. Too many projects failed because of vertical planning and implementation and too much funding was channelled to developing nations that never reached the intended beneficiaries until donors and planners started realising that they were doing something wrong. If they had only involved the beneficiaries from the beginning.

Cultural barriers, as well as attitudes of arrogance about knowledge and vertical practices, have not allowed donors,planners and governments to establish a dialogue with communities of beneficiaries. Indigenous knowledge is at best perceived as an acceptable claim from communities, but rarely considered as one of the main components of development.

Communication has been neglected for too long in development projects, and still is. Even when development organisations and staff realise today that beneficiaries have to be involved, they fail to under- stand that without communication there can be no long-term dialogue with communities. The fact that development projects are mostly in the hands of economists and technicians impedes the understanding of social and cultural issues that are key to a communication strategy.

Too often communication was mistakenly conceived as propaganda or, in the best scenario, as information dissemination, but seldom seen as dialogue. International donors and implementers, governments and NGOs, crave communication when the objective is to gain visibility. Consequently they concentrate on the use of mass media or worse, billboards, paid advertising in journals and generally on media activities that have an impact in the cities, rather than in the poorest rural areas.

There has been an evolution in the concepts of development; nonetheless projects have evolved from not taking communication into account, framing it only as a propaganda or reporting tool. Massive campaigns through mass media, especially for health projects, proved difficult to sustain without permanent funding. Moreover the campaigns have not contributed to establishing dialogue with communities. Since the inception, these projects were exogenous to the beneficiaries and too general to be culturally accepted in countries where cultural and ethnic diversity is high. Development organisations from the United States, that largely promoted the marketing of social goods, had to invest additional funds in self-promotion in order to get attention in developing countries.

The concept of establishing a dialogue with beneficiaries all along the process of conceiving, planning, implementing and evaluating a project has been gradually consolidating. At first, implementers understood that beneficiaries should be involved in the activities leading to social and economic development of a community, for the purpose of building up a sense of ownership within the community. This was at last perceived as important especially in terms of the sustainability of the project once the external inputs ended.

Next, planners realised that the sense of ownership couldn't be promoted if the beneficiaries didn't have a word in the decisions made before a particular project started. For example, the simple issue of deciding where to dig a borehole and place a hand pump could reveal the complexity of internal relations within a rural community.

Technical people that had often seen communities as a homogenous human universe went through a learning process that helped them realise that a community as the society at large is also a composite of interest groups, rich and poor, whose cultural complexity has to be understood beforehand.

The concept of participatory development has lead to a greater level of understanding of the role of communication for development. More projects now include communication staff and budget funds specifically assigned to communication activities. This has also revealed the lack of trained communicators for development; actually, this specialty seldom exists in universities. Among the thousands of academic institutions that produce journalists, only a very few offer training for people interested in communication for development.

It seems there are more than 300 communications schools in Latin America, training over 120,000 students. Most of these training centres aim to prepare communications professionals for the mass media,the advertising industry, the so-called business communications and public relations.

There is not one single school of communications really training communicators for development, scientific communicators or pedagogiccommunicators. In part, that is the very reason why we find such a distressing situation in the field of communication for development. It is very difficult to understand the reason why that type of communications school and university faculties continue to proliferate while there are not enough jobs for the newly graduated. Our society needs schools that form another kind of communicator, those that do not exist right now, at least not in the quantities that are needed.

Communicators for development are a rare species. Most of those that correspond to such a profile are self-made communicators coming from other disciplines, who turned to communications because they identified the real need by working on development projects. Agronomists, sociologists, rural extension workers and facilitators have turned into much better development communicators than journalists which are often too biased towards mass media and vertical practices.

One very important obstacle for including participatory communication components in development projects is the donors' need for scale, which either paralyses cooperation or leads to gigantic and artificial projects that result in equally resounding failures. White elephants as we refer in Spanish to those expensive and gigantic projects that never move have done much more harm than good to developing countries. The issue of scale is often related to the donor's political agenda and internal administrative regulations rather than to development needs. The requirements of proving success in the short-term or measuring a project in numbers of beneficiaries, while excluding qualitative aspects and long-term benefits, have lead to projects that are only successful while funding is available. In a more reasonable framework for development, scale would have to do with linking communities with similar issues of concern and facilitating exchanges, instead of multiplying models that clash with culture and tradition.

The macro level is often a trap in a world diverse in cultures and rich in differences. Going to scale is not always the right long-term solution and massive models cannot replace bottom-up networking. The international donor community is still reluctant to acknowledge 3 or 40 years of failures and millions down the drain because of ill-planned macro programmes. The eagerness to go fast, to show short-term results, and to extend coverage to large numbers of people has actually backfired.It has also distorted the role of communication, which has been largely misused for the purpose of institutional visibility, and seldom as a development device. Mass media has been privileged over other communication tools, with the results that we know: enormous investments, which do not leave anything at the grassroots level once the technical assistance and the funding are withdrawn.

If real changes are expected in the way communication is applied in development projects, we first need to see changes inside the donor and implementing organisations. Those changes could involve using communication strategies from the initial stages of planning a programme or project for example, by allocating a fixed percentage of the total budget to communication activities. Also, changes are needed that will affect the profile of the project staff by incorporating development communicators rather than publicists, and sociologists rather than journalists. Maybe at some point we will all understand better that macro is not just a matter of mega, but also a matter of participation of the intended beneficiaries.And participation has never been massive if it is driven from the top.

Some progress has been made, though not enough, in terms of gradually involving beneficiaries at the planning and implementing stages of a project. However, the evaluation of programmes and projects is still a donor driven exercise, which remains external and vertical to the beneficiaries. Surprisingly enough, the whole evaluation system seems totally outdated to deal with participatory development; nevertheless it is still very strongly present. Other than the fact that institutions specialised in doing evaluations represent an industry by itself, there is another reason that explains its current predominance: by contracting private evaluators donors keep control over evaluations. If we look at it rationally, there are important contradictions in the manner most evaluations are done today, and the main contradiction is that beneficiaries are cut off from the process, seen only as objects of study and not subjects that can contribute to the evaluation process. The following are some aspects that obscure the results of many evaluations.

First of all, the fact that donors and/or implementers sponsor the evaluations of their own projects has an impact on the quality of results; evaluators are likely to be biased to a lesser or larger extent since they depend on future contracts with the same or similar organisations.

Second, who decides on the very objectives of an evaluation? Who will mainly benefit from the evaluation: is it the beneficiaries or the organisation that contracts it? The objectives of evaluations usually respond to institutional agendas.

Third, evaluations are often done by experts with little knowledge about the cultural, political and social context, nor do they speak the language; these are mainly consultants from private companies based in the United States or Europe. Very few projects hire national or Third World consultants with a background that facilitates a higher understanding of local culture. Occasionally United Nations development agencies exchange south-south consultants for this purpose, which is already an improvement.

Fourth,the battery of evaluation instruments is usually taken from already existing models. It's usually adapted for a particular project without sufficient consultation with the grassroots communities and with little consideration of cultural aspects.

Fifth, for statistical purposes, most of the evaluations avoid open questions and concentrate on checklist type formats that aim to obtain numbers and percentages as opposed to qualitative assessments.

Finally, the timing of evaluations is habitually donor driven and has no relevance to really measuring the benefits of a project to the community. Often evaluations are done just by the conclusion of an institutional intervention, thus capturing a picture of the development process at its best moment.

The type of information that an evaluation may bring is often of more use to the implementers than to the beneficiaries. Problems of inaccuracy of information may also obscure the results and interpretation. Inaccuracy is not only related to the inputs for example in relation to an AIDS campaign but often with the lack of knowledge on the culture and forms of organisation of respondents. The evidence that evaluators are looking for, may be distorted by the existing gap between the evaluators and the community.

The bottom line is that the evaluation process should also integrate dialogue as an essential tool. The whole concept of evaluation is to be reassessed. During the past decades we have finally moved towards the concept of people-centred development and towards a people-centred communication model. It is time to move towards people-centred evaluation models. This has happened already at the grassroots level in some of the most interesting examples of participatory communication. During their four decades of growth and development, there were no formal external evaluations of the Bolivian miners' radio stations; but the fact is that their constituency constantly and permanently evaluated the stations and actually directed the process through continuous dialogue. Honest and useful evaluations will only be possible when donors and implementers are ready to surrender their institutional agendas.

Radio

For more than fifty years radio has been the most appealing tool for participatory communication and development. It is without a doubt the communication tool most widely spread throughout the world and has always been the ideal medium for change. Radio had much to do with the changes in the communication landscape of

Europe since the early 1970s when the radio libre or pirate stations popped up by the hundreds in Italy,France and other countries of the conservative continent. Radio Tomate and the others that started in small clandestine rooms of Paris or Milan may have evolved to successful commercial enterprises over the years, but the whole spectrum of radio and television in Europe has changed since their creation.

In the mid-40s, about three decades before diversity in electronic media would spread, small and often isolated communities of campesinos (poor farmers) or miners in Latin America had already started operating their own stations, not only to challenge the monopoly of state media, but also to have, for the first time, a voice of their own.

The social struggles of the 1960s and 1970s, the resistance to military dictatorships that were delivered to power courtesy of the CIA, contributed to the multiplication of independent and community- based radio stations by the thousands. Today, any small country in Latin America can count by hundreds the stations, most of them FM, that serve rural or urban communities with content, that is appropriate to the local language, culture and needs.

Individually, most of these radio stations, often housed in a school, a church or a union building, may not make waves that reach far, but the ensemble certainly has the power of a tsunami. They have rocked down governments and launched new populist leaders. But above all, they have served their constituency on a daily basis, without much noise, mostly open to people's ideas and voices.

Asia and Africa are certainly undergoing the same process that Latin America lived through decades ago. As people repudiate the last dictators, the new voices emerge from various media, and radio is usually in the forefront. As soon as the state monopoly cracks down, small organisations and communities lift their antennas over the villages. Asia provides important examples in the Philippines, Sri Lanka and Nepal, while in Africa several countries are taking advantage of the new democratic winds, the example of South Africa being outstanding among them.

The smallest and most precarious community radio station already makes a difference for a community. The presence of a community radio station, even if it is not highly participatory, has an immediate effect on the population. Small stations usually start airing music for most of the day, thus making an impact on cultural identity and community pride. The next step, closely associated with music programming, is carrying announcements and dedications which contribute to the strengthening of the local social networks. When the station grows in experience and skill, local production of health or education-related programmes starts. These contribute to share information on important issues that affect the community.

Community radio stations have multiplied by the thousands all over the world over the past five decades. It is almost impossible to even calculate the real numbers, as statistics do not include the many that operate without a legal license. Essentially they are important within their own community geographic and social universes, though once in a while the names of some of these stations are heard across the borders: Radio Enriquillo in Dominican

Republic, Radio La Voz de la Montaña in Mexico, Radio Animas in Bolivia, Radio Qawinakel in Guatemala, Radio Xai-Xai in Mozambique, Radio Tubajon in the Philippines, Radio Sagarmatha in Nepal, Katutura Community Radio in Namibia, Kagadi-Kibaale Community Radio in Uganda, Chikaya Community Radio Station in Zambia.

The process of communicating through radio has gone through various stages during the past five decades. Radio has been instrumental for social change and moreover,has invented participatory communication, as we know it today. The first to appear in October 16, 1947, was Radio Sutatenza in Colombia. Established by José Joaquin Salcedo Guarin, a Catholic priest, the station had two main objectives: to broadcast the Christian doctrine to poor farmers and to teach skills that would contribute to community development. Radio Sutatenza grew steadily over the decades until the powerful Cadena Caracol bought it in the early 1990s.

Participation in community radio stations varies from total ownership to different degrees of audience involvement in programming and management. The classic example of total ownership and control of a radio station by its constituency is the network of miners' radio stations in Bolivia. Having been established since 1949, this network is one of the first experiences and one of the most outstanding examples of popular and participatory communication in the world. It is not often that we encounter radio stations that have been conceived, set up, managed, technically run, financed and maintained by the community. Furthermore, the miners' radio stations are also the paradigm of a communication initiative that is part of a larger political and social change project. Last but not least, the fact that at its peak in the 1970s the miners' radio network was comprised of as many as 26 independent stations, which is not negligible at all in terms of scale. Unfortunately, we won't find many other examples of this level of quality.

In recent years we have some other examples of stations where community ownership is an important feature, such as Radio Izcanal in El Salvador and the local radio stations in Burkina Faso, formerly known as High Volta, and Haiti. In the last two examples, the stations were actually set up with both external funds and technical assistance. In Burkina Faso the project of creating six local radio stations was a result of the vision that Thomas Sankara had when he was still Minister of Information, even before he became President and changed the name of the country.

The whole project started collapsing when he was ousted and killed by his close friend and arms companion, Blaise Campaore. In Haiti in 1994, United Nations Educational Scientific and Cultural Organization (UNESCO) donated radio equipment and provided initial training for four stations in remote areas of the island, but the stations are still struggling to build their own identity in a country constantly shaken by political upheaval.

Networking has always been a challenge for community-based communication projects. Top-down networking can easily be done by commercial ventures because of the highly centralised organisation, but that doesn't work as easily when dealing with a group of independent radio stations, each one owned by a different community. Maybe the first question to answer is what defines a network? The miners' radio stations of Bolivia were not considered a network because they aired the same programmes or had a central management, but because they were capable of linking their signals when it was judged necessary, and they pursued the same objectives: to improve the life of Bolivian miners and be heard by the whole nation.

The other example of networking that is worth mentioning is Tambuli in the Philippines. These stations, around twenty, were set up with the help of external technical assistance and funding from UNESCO and Danish International Development Agency (DANIDA). Some aspects of networking include exchanges of cassettes, training, meetings and overall monitoring from the Tambuli Foundation in Manila. But in terms of linking their signal or exchanging material in real-time, no networking is possible as the stations are spread out in the most remote places of the island and can't possibly get in touch through their low-powered transmitters. Technically, Tambuli is not a network, although philosophically all the stations share the same objectives and ideas.

The Local Radio Network in Indonesia shows radio networking is possible even when the stations that make up the network are all privately owned. Again, this is an example of the diversity that we have found during the research process. It is essential to understand the political context of Indonesia in order to appreciate the relevance of this network to communication for social change. There is simply no other community radio in Indonesia. No law provides for such, and after decades of Suharto's strong military regime, it will still take some time until new legislation on communication is established. Albeit, the need for democratic communication inspired UNESCO to support more than twenty private local radio stations, small stations with little resources of their own, and to spark a process of networking with the help of new technologies.

UNESCO provided additional equipment, training and technical assistance so the stations would start producing and airing local news and locally produced programmes. Computers and Internet access enable the stations to exchange news on a daily basis, thus consolidating the networking process. In spite of threats by the army, especially in politically hot regions as Ache, the network continues to grow. On a much larger scale, Púlsar is a news agency in Latin America that provides daily reports and news through e-mail and the Internet, to several hundreds of community radio stations. From a networking perspective, Púlsar has been successful in establishing a system of correspondents all over Latin America and the Caribbean, who provide daily feeds and news from people's perception.

Madagascar is following a model similar to the Tambuli stations, with its radio stations in Fianarantsoa and Morondava. These two stations a third is likely to be established in Antananarivo were set up with support from Switzerland's Développement et Cooperation (DDC), with the objective of serving rural communities in their respective geographical areas of influence. This may not be an example of networking because of the lack of contact among the stations, but may become an example of ownership by the community. During the first two years efforts were directed to establish the two stations as community media,. the first stations of their kind in Madagascar. Next, the process is scheduled to transfer total ownership of the stations to the rural associations currently represented on the management board. However, there is much uncertainty as to what will happen when Swiss technical assistance totally withdraws.

Among the most relevant experiences of radio stations that have succeeded in establishing themselves as examples of participatory communication for social change, those originated by Catholic priests are in the forefront. From the first community radio station ever, Radio Sutatenza, to the thousands that operate today mainly in Latin America, radio has been the most supportive medium of communities struggling for a better world. The Catholic priests behind these communication projects quickly understood that the survival and development of the radio stations had to be linked to community participation, involving the real social, political and cultural needs of the people, and not just to preaching about faith or against communism. A classic example comes from the mining districts of Bolivia. Early in the fifties a group of Catholic priests established Radio Pío XII in Llallagua, with the objective of fighting communism and alcoholism among miners, exactly as Radio Sutatenza did a few years before in rural Colombia. Soon after, the station moved so close to the miners' community, that it joined the network of union radio stations. In subsequent years it was often attacked by the army, and literally, under fire, exactly as the other stations and for the same reasons defending the political and social rights of workers. Radio San Gabriel in La Paz, which focused mainly on its peasant constituency, has grown to become one of the most important national radio stations in Bolivia.

Several radio stations functioning under the umbrella of the Tambuli network in the Philippines, are actually supported at the grassroots level by priests and pastors, such as Radio Tubajon and Radio Loreto both located on Dinagat Island, north of Mindanao. Radio Quillabamba in Peru and Radio Huayacocotla in Mexico, are among the group of outstanding examples of radio stations supported by progressive priests, entirely identified with the local population.

It is not unusual to find community radio stations that have been set up with support from local or international NGOs, but it is less common to find radio stations that were established by government institutions in order to serve the community.

There are few of the latter and usually when these stations exist it is more often the result of good-willed individuals challenging the system, rather than as an expression of government policy to provide a voice for the people. What Thomas Sankara did during the early 1980s in Burkina Faso has not been replicated by other African governments, who have been too jealous to release their tight control over the media.

The Mexican government, on the other hand, does have a policy of promoting community radio, in particular within indigenous communities. Radio Margaritas is one of the 24 indigenous radio stations established by the Instituto Nacional Indigenista (INI), an official institution. These stations produce and air programmes in 31 local languages and Spanish, and reach an estimated six million indigenous Mexicans.

As with some other interesting projects from Mexico, the stations are the fortunate result of political contradictions, and precisely because these contradictions are far from being resolved, the stations have survived through various changes of government. Radio Kiritimati in the Kiribati archipelago in the South Pacific and Kothmale Radio in Sri Lanka are also examples of community radio stations that were established and are partly funded by the government, with little political interference.

Kothmale Radio is an experience worth describing because it is one of the first projects aiming at the convergence between radio and the Internet. Equipped with computers and Internet access, the station receives requests for information from the audience, searches the web for the appropriate data, and returns the results to the listeners, in local language. It is also building a database with information useful to the local constituency. As a tool for social change and participatory communication, radio has several comparative advantages over the other media.

First, it is cost-efficient in terms of investment both for those that run the station and for the audience.

Second, it is pertinent in terms of language and content ideal for the huge illiterate population that still remains marginalised especially in rural areas of the Third World.

Third, it is relevant to local practices, traditions and culture.

Fourth, once the initial investment in equipment is made, sustainability is feasible, though dependent on the level of community participation.

Fifth, in terms of outreach and geographic coverage radio has a strong advantage over other media.

Last but not least, the convergence between radio and the Internet is providing new strength to community radio and has enormously increased networking opportunities.

Video

Video, as a communication tool for development and social change, has always been the subject of comparisons and disputes among the film and the television industries. In order to gain its own identity, the video tool for development had to differentiate itself from the broadcasting system, which is mostly driven by commercial interests. For many years video has been the poor relative of the well- established film and television industries. It has been perceived as a marginalised and low-quality desperate attempt to compete with the commercial networks. Because of the cost of running a television station, most independent projects that aim to promote culture or social issues through television are condemned to have a short life. Even in industrialised nations,the so-called cultural networks or public broadcasting has a hard life.

During the 1960s and 1970s a few attempts were conducted in Latin America to establish alternative television stations in countries such as Bolivia or Chile. None was successful over the years. At one point, each university in Bolivia had its own television channel offering cultural programming, debates and news from a different perspective. But it proved to be unsustainable and as soon as commercial licenses became accessible through bidding, the university television channels faded off. In Chile, as in some other countries, university television channels just had to compete commercially with the others, so little time was left for social and cultural programmes. On the other hand, independent video networks have managed to survive by revealing a social reality that is seldom seen in television. In spite of peoples' tastes having been moulded by the commercial offerings of television and cable networks, independent video is still alive and well. Somewhere within this process, as technology became more affordable and easier to manipulate, video grew as a separate communication tool, with its own comparative advantages over television.

The uses of video in social development projects show a great deal of creativity and capacity to adapt to the changing cultural and social context. In third world countries video is now embraced in much the same manner as radio was by the previous generation, as a tool to support education, cultural identity, organisation and political participation. Many innovative participatory video experiences have developed all over the world. Video SEWA in India, the Kayapo Indians in Brazil, FAWO in South Africa, New Dawn in Namibia, Television Serrana in Cuba, TV for Development in Uganda, CESPAC in Peru, the Capricorn Video Unit in Zimbabwe, Video & Community Dreams in Egypt, and Nutzij in Guatemala, among many others.

Video SEWA (India) among the video-based experiences, is one of the best demonstrations of the participatory potential that this communication tool can unleash. It is also one of the first and long- lasting video experiences in the world. It all started in 1984 when the late Martha Stuart, an international video communications consultant and founder of Martha Stuart Communications, travelled to India and conducted a video training workshop in Gujarat for twenty women, mostly illiterate, from the Self-Employed Women's Association (SEWA).

The seed that was planted in the right place at the right moment has become an important tool within SEWAs social and organisational work. Among the important outcomes of this experience is the fact that women with almost no formal education were capable of assimilating the video tool, and their role in society immediately changed as a result. Martha Stuart's children, Sarah Stuart and Barkley Stuart, continued the work of their late mother by supporting similar projects in Nigeria and Egypt.

Some of the earliest, best and bigger experiences of participatory video were promoted by Food and Agricultural Organization (FAO) and, ironically enough, with the acquiescence of governmental institutions. This is the case for Centro de Servicios de Pedagogia Audiovisual para la Capacitacion (CESPAC) in Peru in 1975, Programa de Desarrollo Rural Integrado del Trópico Humedo (PRODERITH) in Mexico in 1978, and more recently Centre de Services de Production Audiovisual (CESPA) in Mali in 1989.

The three were inspired by Manuel Calvelo, a communication specialist who had enormous influence in establishing the guidelines for participatory communication projects in Latin America. Two Peruvian communicators that had been trained by Calvelo in CESPAC, in fact, provided technical assistance to the Mali experience. These projects are a live illustration of how individuals are determinant in defining the spirit of participatory projects: Manuel Calvelo at the field level and Colin Fraser in FAO headquarters were instrumental in supporting what may have been considered expensive and weird projects by development officials both in FAO and government institutions.

Among all the other United Nations organisations FAO has been the leading agency in terms of developing the concept of communication for development, followed by UNESCO which has mostly supported community radio initiatives. The United Nations Children's Emergency Fund (UNICEF), in spite of having the largest communication staff at the field level, has not been able to sustain a direction where participatory communication would be central to field activities.

Following the death of former Executive Director James Grant in 1995, philosophical changes took place within UNICEF. The result was that most of UNICEF's budget now goes to fundraising campaigns and short-term impact activities. The other UN agencies barely count in terms of promoting participatory communication projects and having a long- term vision.

FAO not only supported long-term communication projects that contributed to build a national capacity, but also developed, at the same time, a conceptual framework through seminars, international meetings, and a wealth of publications. The information and communication cluster at FAO headquarters worked best under the direction of Colin Fraser and, later in the 1980s, Silvia Balit.

The administrative reorganisation of FAO in the mid-90s,with the relocation of staff, departments and resources, seems to have affected the vision on communication for development that was prevalent in earlier years.

Both CESPAC (Peru)and PRODERITH (Mexico), as well as CESPA (Mali)more recently, are related to agricultural development and peasant organisations. The projects had a strong component of training and video which was initially utilised as a visual tool to spread technical innovations in farming and livestock management. Very soon the peasants themselves voiced the need to also focus on social needs such as strengthening community organisation.

This evolution coincided with rapid improvements in video technology during the 1980s: cheaper, smaller and lighter hand-held cameras with built-in batteries and cassette tapes. Video became the ideal tool to facilitate a dialogue between the community and the technical staff, and a means to exchange knowledge horizontally.

The video products (video documentaries or video lessons)still remained an important output of these projects (PRODERITHs catalogue lists several thousand productions), but making the video items became increasingly important, as it involved a process of collective reflection and dialogue on each topic.

Using video as a participatory tool and emphasising the process rather than the product are key concepts in the work of Maneno Mengi a group based in Zanzibar since the mid-90s. Maneno Mengi (many words in Kiswahili) is actually an NGO that specialises in low-cost digital video production, in support of social development initiatives. Its work has benefited fisher folks as well as peasants of Tanzania. Maneno Mengi uses the video camera as a mirror for communities to scrutinise their problems and find solutions. The process can last for several months, on a daily basis. The video camera participates in community discussions; the recorded segments are shown once and again to the community or to relevant authorities if needed. After several months, when social changes are already taking place, the material is edited, mostly as a summary of the whole process.

Community representatives participate in the editing sessions, which are simplified with the use of computer laptops loaded with video editing software. Looking at the ensemble of video-based communication experiences, we can categorise three distinct perspectives: those for which the process before the video product is essential,those for which the video product itself is the end result, and those that emphasise the process after the video product is completed. Certainly these distinctions are not too rigorous, but they allow us to better understand the strengths of each communication initiative. TV

Maxambomba and TV Viva in Brazil, as well as Teleanalisis in Chile, are examples that show the impact of video after production is completed. This is not to say that these groups do not care about the production process, but they certainly are outstanding because of the way they relate to audiences.

The experience of Teleanalisis has long ago folded; nonetheless it had an enormous social impact in Chile during the 1970s and 1980s, under the strong Pinochet regime. Teleanalisis was an alternative for news systematically censored in Chilean television under the dictatorship. Aggressive cameramen went out to record peoples' demonstrations, political repression, and a variety of social problems. The material was edited in secret and copied to VHS cassettes, which were distributed through clandestine unions, religious organisations, and community groups.

TV Viva and TV Maxambomba in Brazil operate in a different context, a democracy where media is owned by large economic groups, among the most influential in Latin America, such as TV Globo. Both TV Viva (from Recife,Brazil, in the North), and TV Maxambomba (from Rio de Janeiro, Brazil), struggle to offer the marginalised neighbourhoods another image of Brazil, an image that takes into account the problems, the needs, and the overall expression of the local community.

In spite of their names, neither is a television station. Their video production touches upon all kinds of issues that can be of interest to the community: politics, health, sexuality, unemployment, education, black culture, citizen's rights and the environment. Humour is an important ingredient that helps to attract audiences. In the streets and open places of Olinda or Nova Iguaçu, TV Viva and

TV Maxambomba deploy their giant screens to project video shows that attract people by the hundreds. It?s public entertainment and at the same time educational. Viewing is no longer a passive activity for the activists of TV Viva and TV Maxambomba.

Television Serrana in Cuba, is a distinctive experience because it takes place in a country where the government has always had a stronghold on the media. However, it is also a country where film, video and the arts in general have enjoyed great support from the state. The main film festival in Latin America takes place every December in Havana and includes important video selections. Cuban independent video production groups have multiplied over the last decade and have their own national festival.

What makes Television Serrana different is that the group has established itself in one of the most isolated regions of the island, the Sierra Maestra, famous for being the guerrilla stronghold during the late fifties. Television Serrana looks at the social situation of the peasant population and provides an opportunity for local communities to voice their concerns and expectations. Particularly successful items are the video-letters, mostly made with children and addressed to other children in Cuba and the world.

Though video, as a participatory communication tool for social change, is still at the beginning of its journey, the potential is huge particularly because of the forthcoming convergence with Internet- based visual applications. At present, the ratio between video and radio in social change experiences is, perhaps, one to fifty, but this could change over the next decade as Internet connections speed-up and hard drive memory becomes cheaper.

Video has its own comparative advantages that are worth mentioning.

First, new digital technologies are making it more affordable, easier to handle, and very competitive with professional formats in terms of quality; video is no longer a poor relative of television.

Second, the potential of using video within the framework of an interactive and dialogic process, and still having a video product at the end is an enormous advantage. The instant playback feature of video is one of its most empowering qualities; it enables continuous participation and immediate feedback. This dimension allows those who are the subject and those who operate the technology to collaborate as equals.

Third, building on the classic adage one image is worth a thousand words, the power of visuals in communication is more extensive every day. Images are trustworthy (even if we know they can be manipulated); visuals easily motivate people.

Finally, the convergence with Internet-based technologies is very promising.

Theatre

In a world dominated by electronic media, where television antennas can be counted by the thousands even in the poorest shanty towns and where the profiles of satellite dishes emerge even in the middle of the desert community theatre has not only survived, but has an important role in communicating for development. Theatre, puppets, dance and music are firmly rooted in the traditional cultural and artistic expressions of manv communities in poorer countries. It is difficult to imagine a community that has completely forgotten any of these forms of collective participation and entertainment.

Sometimes the tradition is only sleeping, it has been neglected because of other urgencies (like survival in the globalised world), but it can be instantly revived when a new motivation arises. The old rich costumes set aside through several generations come out from the wooden trunks where they were carefully folded; the colourful masks and puppets glow again under the sun; the drums or locally made marimbas or balofon regain their clear sounds. The tradition of expressing the local history and the dreams of a community through music, dance or theatre are alive and well even in the most isolated places on earth. And that is precisely why the communication projects that aim to build on traditional forms of expression have many chances to succeed.

There are several reasons for choosing theatre or puppets or dance as a means of communicating for development and encouraging community participation. The first, and more obvious, is that it's already there at the community level, and it's most appreciated by people. Another reason is that in spite of electronic media being almost everywhere nowadays, very little is there content-wise that can help communities improve their quality of life or to organise themselves better. If only entertainment were not only entertainment.

At least radio, compared to television, makes a major effort to reach communities in their own local languages, but too often the contents of programming is detached from local needs and from local cultural identity overall. Many of the drama-based experiences that we know of in the world were established because the available media either were not accessible to the people, or were not responding to their needs for information and communication.

The network of popular theatre in Nigeria was born to serve areas of the country where not even national or state radio, let alone television, had coverage. In the early 1990s UNICEF realised that the investment in radio and television campaigns had little influence in zones of Nigeria where communities lived in complete isolation from any form of electronic-based information. Moreover, the very impact of the radio and television strategy over other areas of the country was in question. The establishment of small drama groups at the level of local governments greatly contributed to support health and education activities with innovative means of communication, using the most important local resources: people, culture, tradition and language. The proliferation of these groups was challenging in terms of scale and the impact on the population could be evaluated immediately, because of the face-to-face communication that was implemented. Scripts on the most important health issues were developed and locally adapted to each particular context.

In Nepal, the Aarohan Theatre has been promoting community theatre since 1988. Although the troupe is not based in a specific community, it has placed its technical capacity at the service of training local drama groups who would in turn develop scripts and plays to support local participation for social change.

Over the years a network of some thirty groups have been established with the help of Aarohan, some in very remote areas of Nepal. Travelling theatre groups supportive of community participation and social change are also well established in the South Pacific, such as Wan Smolbag in Vanuatu or the Awareness Community Theatre (ACT) in Papua, New Guinea.

Theatre is also important to promote social change in urban settings. The examples of Teatro Kerigma in Colombia, Nalamdana in India and Teatro Trono in Bolivia are illustrative of this trend. Street theatre has a variety of forms, including one-man performances and mimes to more organised drama groups. Teatro Trono was initially established by street children and youths in El Alto city, on the outskirts of La Paz, Bolivia. It eventually became a larger cultural group and expanded its activities to other urban areas of Bolivia. Puppets have also been used as a tool for social change in many countries, particularly in India and Indonesia. Among the puppeteer?s groups there is much diversity of technique, topic and audiences. Adults benefit from it as well as children. String puppets, glove puppets, shadow puppets and rod puppets are some of the traditional techniques employed, but in recent years computer-controlled puppetry is being introduced in film studios and on television shows.

Various puppeteers' troupes are concerned about AIDS prevention, such as Puppets Against AIDS in Namibia (PAAN), active since 1995, Dadi Pudumjee in India, and Nyanga Tshabalala in South Africa. In Hong Kong, The Kids on the Block a troupe of large-sized puppets, has specialised in educating children on issues of discrimination against children with disabilities.Some puppeteers are using television to broaden their audiences, although this has an impact on the quality of perception and participation. Using the national language, Tagalog, the Batibot Puppet Show in the Philippines is designed to help pre-school children from low- income families develop skills and values through entertainment.

The Si Unyil Puppet series in Indonesia has been on television since the early 1980s. Similarly, the Puppet Theatre of Ardeshir Keshavarzi (Iran) and Uncle Sargam by Farooq Qaisar (Pakistan) are popular shows in their respective countries. It is difficult to evaluate how many of these puppet shows really deal with social change and how much of what they broadcast is plain entertainment for children. It is obvious that the ill-defined television audience forces puppeteers to address culture and content in very general rather than specific terms, without having the possibility of establishing a real dialogue with the audience.

The Lilac Tent is an amazing experience taking place in Bolivia, inspired in various performing arts and housed under a huge circus travelling-tent. The project, which aims to positively affect the sexual behaviour of Bolivian youth and prevent AIDS and STDs, is a mixture of entertainment and educational activities. The Lilac Tent is something like a medieval circus combined with modern educational techniques. Wherever it travels, it certainly captures the attention of the whole community.

Outside the tent people can watch video documentaries on health issues, puppet performances or evening music shows; while inside The Lilac Tent and organised in groups of ten,the visitors have the opportunity of participating in a series of instructive activities and games. Though funded by United States Agency for International Development (USAID) and technically supported by the communication cluster at Johns Hopkins University (JHU), this project has evolved much beyond the usual social marketing model.

Theatre and puppets as tools of participatory communication for social change have comparative advantages, particularly in live performances that are not filtered by television.

First above all,is the cultural relevance, especially when local troupes are in charge. Traditional values are preserved and strengthened, and communicating in the local language contributes to the process of community participation.

Second, is cost-effectiveness and the potential of immediately having an impact and appreciating this impact on the audience.

Third, is the advantage of establishing a live dialogue that may derive in a learning process, both for the audience and the drama group.

Finally, the entertainment factor, which enables the contents to be conveyed, channels the energies of the audience, through surprise or through laughter, to the processes of comprehension and participation.

The Internet

Although often perceived as the future of communications, the Internet is already here and represents a presence that is still unchanged in terms of its potential benefits for social change.Because of its own nature as the product of scientific research and intellectual development, the Internet has received much more attention from scholars than any other medium for development. While the actual experiences of the Internet as a tool for social change are only two or three years old, the number of evaluations and studies is far ahead of this reality.

The willingness to make the Internet a useful tool for social development and social change leads to many assumptions and idealisations. Much is said about the potential benefits, while most of it is yet to be realised. Somehow, this competition towards defining on paper (actually, mostly through e-mail discussions and Web-based debates) what the Internet should be is a legitimate reaction to the fact that the Internet is already something which does not correspond to what we would prefer.

The very evolution of the Internet is amazing. First it was a U.S. national security project, then a noble tool for democratising information exchanges, finally a gigantic virtual worldwide supermall. The military lost it to computer wizards and scientists at the beginning; the well-intentioned scholars lost it more recently to globalisation and advertising.

In terms of what the Internet represents for social change in developing countries, a reality check shows a mostly dim picture. The United States has more computers than the rest of the world combined. Currently, around 50 percent of the Internet users are in the U.S.; about 25 percent are in Europe; and only 12-13 percent are in Asia. South Asia, with 23 percent of the world's people, has less than one per cent of the world's Internet users.

The typical Internet user worldwide is male, less than 35 years old, with a university education and high income, urban-based and English speaking a member of a very elite minority. In a world with thousands of languages and cultures, 9 percent of Web-based information is in English. The ten other most important languages in the world are largely under-represented within the remaining 1 percent, including Spanish, which has more speakers than English worldwide.

The pattern is similar in terms of content. U.S. Web sites largely dominate, and consequently, the content is mainly of interest to U.S.-based users. A peasant in India or a factory worker in Brazil, just to name two important and populated countries in the Third World, will not find much of interest on the current World Wide Web, even when he or she gets around fairly well in English.

Certainly, we could say the same about television. Cable and satellite TV have flattened the landscape of television worldwide. The same concept of television, the same information, the same feature films or documentaries, the same advertising campaigns are available (or imposed) throughout Asia, Africa, Latin America, Europe and North America. Often the same television channels or Web sites, by the way are available in Spanish, Portuguese or Japanese, but the content is just a mirror image of the original.

Video for social change is new and radically different from commercial television. It is not yet happening on the Internet. There is only one Internet, and it is largely commercial. In terms of the social use which up to now has been a synonym of planting computers in areas previously deprived even of telephone and electricity the existing models are mixed and confusing.

Too many different initiatives are called by the same names, to the point that we don't know any longer what a 'telecentre' is in terms of its social use. Many are just 'cybercafes' for upper middle class students or tourists visiting developing countries. Other telecentres in rural areas are commercial ventures aiming to provide communication services to those that didn't have access before, which as such is not at all a bad thing. These rural telecentres or Internet cabins manage to get telephone land lines or radio and satellite links that are already benefiting community users, who often visit the place to access the phone more than the web. There is clear improvement in terms of access to communications technology, though it is not yet clear if this access will contribute to development and social change or is only a fashionable new gadget.

Many will argue that the introduction of new technologies only widens the gap between the rich and the poor, just exactly as happened in the 1970s with the modernisation programmes. While there had been some success in agricultural, health, nutrition and educational extension programmes, the main beneficiaries were the better-off sections of society. There was little evidence of the hoped for 'trickle down' effect. The diffusion of innovations that was believed to have brought about the Green Revolution, for instance, benefited the richer landowners and farmers.... Indeed, the knowledge gap between the 'haves' and the 'have-nots' has widened as the elites have greater access to the mass media.

In any case new technologies don't seem to frighten away anyone. The technical skills needed are not a barrier for poor and almost illiterate people to access. Knowledge of how to use a computer is not an obstacle in the Third World. Experiences such as El Limón in a small and marginalised village of the Dominican Republic or the hole in the wall in India show that people with no previous computer technology contact whatsoever can easily find their way using the mouse and the keyboard. The 'hole in the wall' is a particularly interesting experiment conducted by Sugata Mitra from the NIIT, which is a multinational company specialising in information technologies and e-commerce: a computer screen and a control stick were placed in the wall of a poor slum.

Within minutes, the children that started playing around with this mysterious object found out how hyperlinks worked, and within a week they had figured out how to write a few words without a keyboard, how to drag and drop documents, and how to browse the Internet. Of course, playing around with a magic box is not the same thing as being able to take advantage of the Internet and finding something useful while browsing the Web. The Web is not yet ready for their needs. Shaping the Internet, or some of it, in a way that serves the objectives of development, democracy, social change and cultural identity through a participatory process may not be easy to achieve, but some are trying hard.

The convergence between radio and the Internet is one of the most interesting symbioses that new technologies can offer. Not only does community radio get empowered to reach new latitudes, but also Internet users learn from a participatory experience that has done much for social change during the past fifty years. The Púlsar network in Latin America, Kothmale Radio in Sri Lanka and the Local Radio Network in Indonesia are some of the relevant examples of this trend.

The Internet has a better chance to succeed as a tool for development and participation if linked to existing communication or information experiences. The Sistema de Información Rural (InfoDes) project in Peru has taken this into consideration when basing its information system on community libraries that were created in rural areas of Cajamarca thirty years ago.

In Colombia, Colnodo is helping existing NGOs and community organisations to build Web sites and make available to others a wealth of information. Similar projects such as Ecuanex (Ecuador), Cabinas Públicas (Peru) and Conectándonos al Futuro (El Salvador) have recently been established. Both Colnodo and InfoDes- as Kothmale Radio in Sri Lanka are aware of the need to develop a local database, designed to make the Internet useful to communities, and not so alienated from local reality. Developing local Web sites, in local languages if possible, could catalyse and renew the interest in the Internet and encourage participation.

In India, the M.S. Swaminathan Research Foundation (MSSRF) is carrying out an experimental project in villages in Pondicherry, about 160 kilometres south of Chennai (formerly Madras). Half the people live below the poverty line earning less than $1 per day. The project, known as 'Knowledge Centre for Sustainable Food Security', is designed to provide information to local rural people according to their needs and demands, using both analogue wireless technologies and dial-up Internet connections. Information is tailored to local needs, especially relating to women and children. Also available to rural families is a directory of government projects, health issues, prices of agricultural produce, information on public events, local transportation schedules, crop insurance projects, and a directory of hospitals and medical practitioners.

The other important condition for success is the linkage of the Internet component to a concrete project of social development. Bangladesh is always surprising everyone with the most creative initiatives. Donors are also pleased to see that most of these are 'in scale' given the size of the country and the population density. Though huge programmes such as Bangladesh Rural Advancement Committee (BRAC) or Grameen Bank may not be replicable in other countries, they provide a wealth of information that can certainly be of use. Though not directly related to the Internet, since 1998 Grameen Bank established a Village Phone System that uses cellular phones to provide access even in the most remote villages. The whole project, which has a commercial component and a social change-oriented objective, is linked to the existing Grameen Bank loan system, which facilitates many aspects. Cellular phones are sold at very low prices to selected Village Phone operators, mostly women. They are in charge of managing the phones as a community service. Accessible prices have been fixed to avoid speculation, and these allow the operators to pay their monthly installments to the bank, to the phone company (Grameen Telecom) and to earn an additional income for their families.

There are various model examples of providing access to the Internet in rural areas of Africa, one of them being particularly interesting, the Nakaseke Multipurpose Community Telecentre in Uganda. Four similar units have been established by a joint UNESCO/ International Development Research Centre (IDRC)/International Telecommunications Union (ITU) project in Mozambique, Tanzania, Mali and Benin. These offer access to computers and the Internet, a fax and a photocopier, a basic library, video shows, newspapers, audio recording, and community listening. The core user groups of Nakaseke MCT are women, youth, teachers, students and local leaders.

A passive use of the Internet may only result in a more homogenised and globalised world, a huge marketplace with many consumers and few products. The potential of the Internet can only be fully explored through a process of occupying spaces and opening windows for local users. The comparative advantages of the Internet look good on paper; however, the challenges in making the Internet a useful tool in places where safe water is unavailable, let alone electricity, are large. Wireless technologies and the convergence with community radio and video, are already signalling the way. But technology alone may not be the answer if culture and identity are not at the heart of the discussion. When new technologies are introduced to a different social setting, what is transferred is not only technology itself, but also the social use of it, a set of assumptions and practices that emerged from another context and other needs.

Challenges of Participatory Communication

WThe history of international cooperation for development is plagued with embarrassing anecdotes that show the extremes reached because of lack of communication: development agents incapable of expressing their technical views and supposed beneficiaries unable to communicate their own perspective. One single example seems to capture the essence of this huge misunderstanding.

Very often in health campaigns that aim to minimise water-borne diseases, women are advised to boil the water before drinking it. This advice, which may seem straightforward, simple to understand, and logical from any point of view, actually symbolises the lack of sensitivity that often characterises development projects.

Radio and television spots with the message "boil the water" continue to be produced and aired in many developing countries regardless of its impact. A female radio producer in Mexico puts it this way: "I tell the ladies over the microphone to boil the water, but I know they're not going to do it, because they have no fuel, they have no wood."

Regardless of the distressing effects of unsafe water, when 8 percent of the rural women in the world depend on wood for cooking and often walk five or more kilometres every day to fetch dry sticks, boiling the water is certainly not a priority for them.

"If community media is the answer what is the question?" The response may be: "the answer is the question." If the questions were more often discussed with the communities, if a permanent and nonexclusive dialogue was established among all stakeholders on local development issues, the question may not have even been formulated.

The questions and the answers on the communication initiatives have to be worked out with the community. What kind of communication does the community need, if any? Which is the communication system traditionally used in the community? What kind of communication tools can the community afford, not only in terms of funding but also in terms of skills and social appropriation of the new media? Participatory research would help to develop these questions and help the community to find the answers.

The dialogic process may also help to demystify the perception of the community as a homogenous human universe. The idealised vision of a community entirely united by its fate or history or culture is one of the first masking myths to go. Every society or community has social strata and divergent interests. Though to different degrees, every community urban or rural has the rich and the poor; the politician and the artist; the religious leader and the fool of the town.

The cultural universe is complex and evolving permanently. Ready made recipes don't work, and technical assistance is only valid through permanent dialogue and communication. Experts in development come and go, and the ideal 'expert', "has to go through these stages: indispensable, necessary, useful and once the initial goals are achieved superfluous", according to Manuel Calvelo.

There is no ideal established model for participatory communication, and each of the case stories confirms the uniqueness of every experience, both with its positive and negative aspects. All had to overcome obstacles, and some couldn't reach the point where external inputs were no longer necessary. We are learning from the virtues and mistakes of these experiences by placing them side-by-side like the pieces of a puzzle, not because at the end of this process there is the complete model for all circumstances, but because from the multiple experiences we may draw some pieces for a new puzzle. If no ideal model is possible, or necessary, still there are some common characteristics of participatory communication that we would like to see more often in those projects and initiatives that claim they have participatory components.

Communication and participation are actually two words sharing the same concept. Etymologically the Latin communio relates to participation and sharing. Modern languages have given different meanings to the word communication it is very often considered synonymous with the word information. There is confusion, mostly by English speakers, between communication the act or process of communicating, and communications with an 's' the means of sending messages, orders, etc. When trying to design the profile of participatory communication, it is important to be conscious about the political implications of participation in development, and moreover of participatory communication:

An issue of power. The democratisation of communication cuts through the issue of power. Participatory approaches contribute to put decision-making in the hands of the people. It also consolidates the capability of communities to confront their own ideas about development with development planners and technical staff. Within the community itself, it favours the strengthening of an internal democratic process.

An issue of identity. Especially in communities that have been marginalised, repressed or simply neglected during decades, participatory communication contributes to install cultural pride and self-esteem. It reinforces the social tissue through the strengthening of local and indigenous forms of organisation. It protects tradition and cultural values, while facilitating the integration of new elements.

The main elements that characterise participatory communication are related to its capacity to involve the human subjects of social change in the process of communicating. The theoretical framework for participatory communication owes much to Paulo Freire. Other models of communication for development, that have been implemented particularly around health issues, often fail to organise their strategy and their values from the perspective of the communities that are the end beneficiaries.

Some of the issues that distinguish participatory communication from other development communication strategies in search of social changes:

— *Horizontal vs. Vertical:* People as dynamic actors, actively participating in the process of social change and in control of the communication tools and contents; rather than people perceived as passive receivers of information and behavioural instructions, while others make decisions on their lives.

— *Process vs. Campaign.* People taking in hand their own future through a process of dialogue and democratic participation in planning communication activities; rather than expensive unsustainable top-down campaigns that help to mobilise but not to build a capacity to respond from the community level to the needs of change.

— *Long-term vs. Short-term.* Communication and development in general is conceived as a long-term process which needs time to be appropriated by the people; rather than short-term planning, which is seldom sensitive to the cultural environment and mostly concerned with showing results for evaluations external to the community.

— *Collective vs. Individual.* Urban or rural communities acting collectively in the interest of the majority, preventing the risk of losing power to a few; rather than people targeted individually, detached from their community and from the communal forms of decision-making.

— *With vs. For.* Researching, designing and disseminating messages with participation; rather than designing, pre-testing, launching and evaluating messages that were conceived for the community, and remain external to it.

— *Specific vs. Massive.* The communication process adapted to each community or social group in terms of content, language, culture and media; rather than the tendency to use the same techniques, the same media and the same messages in diverse cultural settings and for different social sectors of society.

— *People's needs vs. Donors' musts.* Community-based dialogue and communication tools to help identify, define and discriminate between the felt needs and the real needs; rather than donor-driven communication initiatives based on donor needs.

— *Ownership vs. Access.* A communication process that is owned by the people to provide equal opportunities to the community; rather than access that is conditioned by social, political or religious factors.

— *Consciousness vs. Persuasion.* A process of raising consciousness and deep understanding about social reality, problems and solutions; rather than persuasion for short-term behavioural changes that are only sustainable with continuous campaigns.

Community Multimedia Centres

It is widely agreed that information, communication and knowledge cannot remain the preserve of development experts in tackling poverty but must become the basic tools of the poor in improving their own lives. There is equally strong consensus on the dangers of the accelerating inequity of access to knowledge both within and between countries.

Strategies to increase access to knowledge for development need to integrate fully both their approach to the new knowledge resources and their approach to traditional knowledge systems. On the one hand, the introduction of new ICTs into poor or marginalised communities works best when it draws on traditional channels of communication and information, on the reservoirs of indigenous knowledge within the community and on its existing information resources. On the other hand, traditional forms of knowledge acquisition are insufficient to foster an inclusive knowledge society.

People in poor and marginalised communities need access to mechanisms that provide multiple sources of rapid information and information exchange. The Internet and associated technologies are pivotal to the new means of knowledge acquisition. The question is: how should new ICTs and traditional knowledge systems be integrated at the community level in order to maximise the development potential of both? In response to this challenge, UNESCO examined two areas in which it already had a wellestablished track record: long-standing involvement with grass-roots community radio; and more recent involvement with the multipurpose community telecentre. The result of bringing the two together in a novel manner is the Community Multimedia Centre (CMC). This combines community broadcasting with community telecentre facilities and offers a strategy that integrates new and traditional information and communication systems at the local level.

When community radio and new ICTs are actively combined, they offer far greater possibilities for engaging a community in its own development. The possibilities generated by the combination of the two are not confined to quantity or range; the qualitative nature of these possibilities also changes. This is because of the particularly dynamic relationship between communication and information, between contact and content. The combination of a grassroots public platform with access to information highways promotes the public debate and public accountability that are essential for strengthening democracy and good governance. The combination of local radio with a community database developed by local people, building up a store of relevant data for educational, informational and developmental requirements, provides a solid knowledge base for the community and an open learning infrastructure for all its members. It also takes into account the preference of rural communities for a collective assimilation of knowledge, in contrast to the prevailing mode of individual access to Internet.

The CMC is a recent development and the first of its kind, the Kothmale Internet Radio project in Sri Lanka. Kothmale Community Radio (KCR) was set up 20 years ago by the Sri Lanka Broadcasting Corporation when the construction of the Kothmale dam displaced entire villages. Local radio was chosen as a strategy for helping to rebuild the social fabric for those displaced within this rural community and KCR became an important part of many people's lives.

The Kothmale Internet Radio project added a community telecentre facility to the radio station. From the outset, access to Internet was considered both in terms of direct access for members of the community, through training courses or the help of facilitators, and also in terms of indirect access through "radio browsing" programmes. In this way, community radio is used as a gateway for a poor community to actively participate in the global knowledge society through "radio browsing" of websites, by encouraging the use of Internet access at the station and encouraging the use of radio as a platform for public debate.

This approach overturns many assumptions about Internet and related technologies: that they are primarily useful for professionals, business people, academics and students or that they are intrinsically part of a consumer life-style, offering new services almost exclusively in the domain of leisure, entertainment, travel and consumer spending. In Kothmale, radio browsing programmes focus on local economic activities, development and governance issues, culture and entertainment. The daily programmes respond to queries from listeners. Presenters first select relevant, reliable websites and broadcast the programme with local resource persons as studio guests (e.g. doctors for a health programme) who discuss the contents of the mostly English-language sites directly in the national languages. They also describe the websites and explain how they are browsing from one web page to another. Thus, listeners not only get the information they requested, but they understand how it is made available on the web. They can respond to the programme and they know that essential data will remain available in the community database if they wish to make individual use of it. With this daily radio programme, there is continuity within a common learning process encouraging greater inter-activity with and by the community.

The impact of this new way of creating shared meanings and interpretations of information for development is a key marker of the success of the project. The radio programme has triggered a greater interest among community members in receiving information related to poverty alleviation efforts, health, formal and non-formal education, livelihood skills and individual empowerment.

The assumption behind this approach – that Internet can be useful for everyone – was readily taken up by listeners, most of whom had probably no idea that that there could exist a more elitist approach to new ICTs. This echoes the experience of many projects introducing new technologies to poor communities in the developing world:

there are few psychological barriers to overcome among people who have had little or no access to information and communication technologies in any form – new or traditional. A CD-ROM is no more intimidating than an encyclopaedia when one has never used an encyclopaedia.

The Kothmale log book filled by each individual user of the telecentre shows a very wide range of subjects researched by a wide range of users. With an adult literacy rate of 82 percent, Kothmale offers fertile ground for this approach to new knowledge resources. Log book reports vary from one farmer researching information on organic tomato farming to another looking for new varieties of seeds, to a baker seeking new recipes, the local undertaker looking for an on-line funeral business management course, a health worker printing data on mosquito-borne diseases and young people looking for international job opportunities.

The radio browsing programmes have also prompted illiterate people to go online with, for example, an elderly woman seeking the help of a facilitator to visit the site of a sacred Buddhist shrine in India. The radio browsing programmes cater in a similar way for different interest groups. A tea farmer who presents a radio browsing programme found a Tamil-language website explaining new tea drying techniques in southern India and shared this information with the local tea farmers on a browsing programme. Many farmers cultivate bamboo and new uses for bamboo were introduced to Kothmale after a programme browsed a website in the Asia region and found new crafts using bamboo.

When looking at the remarkable ease and speed with which KCR moved into this new, multimedia centre approach, certain pre-existing conditions stand out clearly as having an important impact within the project. The fact that the CMC was built into a wellestablished community radio station with a core professional staff and experienced grassroots volunteer staff meant many development topics were already covered regularly on air and in ways that sought systematically to convey locally-relevant information in context and with a degree of interactivity between listeners and programme makers. Local resource persons with a traditional role as "knowledge-brokers" for the local community had already been identified and mobilised to participate in community broadcasting. Well-adapted local programming by trusted and familiar broadcasters offered an excellent foundation for the introduction of new ICTs. At the same time, high literacy rates and the generalised secondary-school level of education of the younger generations in Kothmale also impacted positively on both the range and the number of people using ICTs.

Building on these favourable conditions, the project strategy of reaching out to the entire community ensured a continuum of information and communication, involving both the spoken and written word, the most educated and the least educated. The daily browsing programmes provide a crucial link between those more likely and those less likely to use ICTs individually. Even those who would never go to the telecentre themselves have a basic understanding of and share a common language to discuss ICTs, because the radio browsing programmes have made cyberspace familiar territory. The clearest illustration of this is the number of cases in which a senior family member has listened to a browsing programme, then encouraged a younger family member to go onto Internet in search of information useful for the small family business.

In Kothmale, there may be a noticeable "generation gap" in terms of individual access to ICTs, but not in terms of appreciating their usefulness. Such positive factors for developing a CMC did not remove the need for carefully planned outreach activities targeting all groups within the community. Those hardest to reach have been young girls. In spite of messages on the radio announcing free training for women and girls, few came from the poorest hamlets of Kothmale. Only door-to-door "canvassing" finally convinced some of the most marginalised women that the training really was meant for them.

One of the lessons of the project has been that proactive gender policies have to be pursued at every level, from targeting women and girls for training opportunities to ensuring that men do not jump the queue for the computers when women are in line. Again, the combination of direct and indirect access to ICTs helps to bridge the gender gap. In Kothmale, 41 percent of telecentre users are women, but they constitute over 50 percent of "radio browsing" users who also interact with new ICTs by telephoning or sending questions to the "radio browsing" producers, then listening to, reacting to and using the information broadcast from the Internet.

Lack of Sinhalese-language materials on-line was a major obstacle, only partly overcome by local efforts to train users to create webpages. Although web skills are so widespread that 40 percent of those making web pages in Kothmale are now peer-taught, only when there are many more "Kothmales" producing their own web pages in Sri Lanka will the lack of locally relevant information in national languages be made good. It is worth noting here that it would take just 50 CMCs in Sri Lanka to ensure that every Sri Lankan is within reach of ICTs and on the right side of the digital divide. The language barrier is less of a problem for Tamil-speakers, thanks to the relatively large number of Tamil-language websites emanating from the large Tamil population of southern India.

At present, the radio browsing formula is the only means to overcome entirely the language barrier, as information on English-language websites is explained and discussed directly in Sinhalese and Tamil. One advantage for Kothmale is the existence of many regionally-based English-language sites carrying a vast range of information relevant for much of the Asian region. The number of school-students at KCR after school hours, surfing the web in English and using English for their email exchanges, indicates that language is far less of a barrier for the younger generations.

Achieving a satisfactory supply of relevant content involves more than the vital matter of identifying and using suitable websites, locally-created or across the Internet. The Kothmale database is building up a collection of useful on-line data, including administrative forms, fact sheets and so forth. On-line governance is a promising future prospect as local and national government documents begin to go online.

The CMC has great potential to evolve into a community learning centre, with a library of multimedia learning materials and access to distance education and training courses just some of the possible uses. Already, two access points at public libraries in nearby towns extend access to Internet to many more users and make the physical link to library collections. Local schoolteachers use the Internet to enrich their lessons and take their classes to visit the centre. Some unplanned outcomes of the project can have a significant impact on contents creation and local use of online resources. The combination of individual and community interaction fosters the emergence of new democratic initiatives with a focus on e-campaigning. A new, active and influential environmental NGO, Green Lanka, germinated from the Internet browsing of some young Kothmale residents who decided to "do something" with their new-found IT resources. Green Lanka must be one of only a few NGOs around the world awarding a national "green label" for exports from headquarters in a village.

The strategy of combining direct and indirect access to new ICTs has also to be assessed in terms of scale and capacity. At present, the number of computers made available to the public through this project is minimal – about six machines in all. While the small telecentre facility and two access points in public libraries can receive up to one or two thousand visits a month, the radio browsing programmes attract many times that number of listeners every day. In this way, a minimal investment in ICT equipment can have an quasiexponential impact within the community. In the future, some local people and, crucially, other local institutions can be expected to acquire their own equipment as usage generates revenue and purchase costs come down. As the number of users increases, it may become commercially viable for small, private Internet kiosks to set up business. There is no reason to believe that any of these developments would obviate the need for or the usefulness of the present system of mass access through radio browsing and the proactive approach to broadbased participation fostered by community telecentre outreach activities.

The CMC formula not only looks set to remain relevant for the medium term, but could become a permanent feature alongside the individual user approach of wealthy consumer societies. As a pioneering pilot project, Kothmale saw a considerable proportion of the project budget allocated to research and evaluation. From the outset, the project was supported by the national authorities and national institutions – with government ministries supplying the dedicated Internet connection, the Sri Lanka Broadcasting Corporation responsible for the radio station and its professional staff, and Colombo University providing technical support for the computers and networks.

This support was important in order to start up a completely new activity in a poor rural area where the level of awareness had not yet created a demand for ICTs. It also needed strong public support for another reason: there was a major credibility barrier to overcome. What did poor, rural people speaking Singhala and Tamil need with Internet? What could justify making ICTs a development priority when there were other, pressing needs? What motivation would people have and would they sustain their interest for any length of time? Today, that battle for credibility has been won and will not need to be fought again – in Sri Lanka, at least.

With the example of Kothmale to build on, it is likely that future CMC projects will follow a somewhat different model: establishing business plans and sustainability strategies from the outset in order to reduce the degree of dependence on public support, reducing the research component as the model becomes more established and networking with each other to pool resources, training and so on. Links with other institutions such as educational and training institutes, development networks or agricultural co-operatives could become a core component of a CMC.

It is conceivable that, as in other countries where broadcast regulations permit it, the community radio component of a CMC could eventually be started up by the community and be fully owned and operated by the community. However, the intrinsic value of building the CMC on an existing local station that is part of the national public broadcaster cannot be overlooked. In the case of Kothmale, the high standard of broadcasting at the station was without a doubt a key to the success of the radio browsing formula. Paradoxically, this model might be of particular interest in those developing countries where chronically under-funded public radios struggle to compete with flourishing new FM stations that are free from public service constraints. By forging a new public service role integrating ICTs, the local stations of national broadcasters could find a new lease of life and benefit from public revenue going into national IT plans.

While in Kothmale the CMC grew from the community radio station, in Timbuktu, Mali, it is the community telecentre that has become the basis for a CMC, with the four radio stations of the town sharing use of a new radio studio within the telecentre. The Timbuktu community telecentre, a pilot project backed by a consortium of partners (UNESCO, IDRC, ITU, SOTELMA (national telecom company), WHO and FAO), opened in April 1999 and was planned as a fairly large-scale infrastructure eventually able to offer specialised services such as telemedicine and distance learning as well as basic services to all members of the community.

UNESCO added the radio equipment to the telecentre in September 2001 in order to enable the local radio stations to make full use of new ICTs and start radio browsing programmes. The local municipal station, Radio Bouctou, and the three private or associative stations,

Radio Alfarouk, Radio Lafia and Radio Jamana run on minimal revenue, equipment and human resources.

Timbuktu and the surrounding area have a far smaller population than Kothmale and an adult illiteracy rate of 50 percent. Its telecentre – three times larger than Kothmale's, with 18 computers – is constantly busy. When this ICT project was proposed and even though the literacy levels, income levels and population density are far lower than in Sri Lanka, there was no credibility barrier to overcome.

Timbuktu suffers from such extreme geographical isolation – with currently just one flight a week made by a 14-seater plane and river boat services taking four days from the capital Bamako – that the contact potential of ICTs was embraced with great enthusiasm from the outset. A remarkable indicator of this support and degree of faith in the benefits of these technologies was the substantial financial contribution made not only by townspeople but by the inhabitants of 43 outlying villages. The telecentre made a series of attempts to encourage the town's radio stations to use its services.

Timbuktu's four radio stations broadcast in a total of six languages to the townspeople and to villages within a 100 km radius. The first users of the community telecentre were not surprisingly the local elite – teachers, office workers, doctors, business people and so on. In order to expand access, a study was made of user needs according to social groups – women, youth, nomadic herders, traders, media etc. – and outreach activities organised. The results were not necessarily what could have been expected: some categories that might have been thought the hardest to reach became aware of the value of ICTs much sooner than, for example, the radio staff of the town.

Several illiterate and semi-literate Touareg camel herders were among the quickest to use the centre in order to open email accounts and deal directly with their tourist clients overseas. While these users now know how to navigate, open their mail box and access their mail with ease, they have to print out each message as they read with great difficulty or only with assistance. Similarly, writing a reply is a difficult task and some use the telecentre emailwriting service. This does not appear to be an obstacle as the total cost is cheap and the message instantaneous.

As a measure of motivation, one Touareg travels 400km about once a month to access his email. If he cannot get a lift with a tourist convoy, this takes him up to a week by camel. This link enables him to run his small tourist guide business and launch projects in his oasis village of Arawane. Most other herders working as guides and using the centre travel in daily from camps some 10 km out of Timbuktu. The hardest-to-reach group – young girls – still forms a minority of users. The single most successful strategy to encourage Internet access among schoolgirls was to find them email pen-friends, mostly from neighbouring countries in French-speaking West Africa. For women's outreach activities, as for those targeting other groups, existing structures were mobilised and local women's associations still provide the key link to the female population.

Most women users are however still from the more privileged groups such as office workers and health workers. Illiterate adults were targeted with great success. Computer-based literacy classes are in demand and three literacy tutors run courses in the telecentre in which they take a discreet, low-profile approach, allowing their "students" to blend in with other computerusers. A self-tutoring literacy software package is currently being finalised. In contrast to the successes of outreach activities for these groups, attempts to attract radio staff initially had significantly lower impact. Only two people working in radio stations came to use the centre spontaneously. The heads of the radio stations or their representatives were first given an introductory course. This was followed by a full basic computer training course given free to two staff members from each station. The telecentre then donated a computer to each station, stipulating that these should be used to train colleagues by those who had followed the basic training course.

Another training session was carried out for radio staff on use of CD-ROMs and the telecentre staff then visited each station, presenting the contents of development CD-ROMs and loading contents onto the stations' computers. Almost a year after these efforts began, the computers in the radio stations were however still visibly under-used and radio staff in a noticeable minority among telecentre users. Usage of the computers in the radio stations appeared to be inhibited by problems of social relations in the workplace: those who now had computer skills were not in a hierarchical position that allowed them to take initiatives with "high-status" equipment – the computer. Only when the telecentre got a high-speed line and was able to offer a good Internet connection did radio staff use of computers pick up.

A free Internet course was given to one staff member per station (offered to those who had not benefited from previous training sessions) and free access to Internet and print-outs of information for programmes offered to all radio staff. At this stage, the first real numbers of radio staff began using the centre, opening email accounts and surfing the web. However, the only radio programmes for which web searches were used regularly concerned sports, music stars and horoscopes. Attempts by the telecentre managers to organise the making of development programmes in the telecentre failed. As in many other parts of the developing world, in Timbuktu development partners –NGOs and IGOs – have been in the habit of paying local radio stations to broadcast development programmes.

Although the development partners may view this as general support for community media, the hard-pressed radio directors naturally enough come to view development programmes as a legitimate source of revenue and are reluctant to use their own resources to make relatively time-consuming, high-input programmes. The radio equipment donated by UNESCO and housed in the telecentre, a Wantok FM radio station-in-a-suitcase, was intended to break this pattern and encourage greater use of Internet by radio staff for making programmes on development issues as part of their regular programming. Training was given in radio browsing techniques: pre-selection of useful websites, advanced search methods, methods of saving or "storing" selected webpages, techniques (for both presenters and resource persons) for describing or visualising web contents and so on. The radio browsing concept was embraced with great enthusiasm by the generally young radio presenters who were eager to use the technique to cover development issues and clearly enjoyed this new dimension of radio presenting, experiencing it as enhancing their role and status as information-brokers. This high level of motivation is crucial as these presenters are paid very little or not at all. With the introduction of the suitcase radio, their use of the telecentre immediately rose.

However, none of the radio staff had sufficiently good web browsing skills to be able to prepare browsing programmes with ease after the initial, limited number of training sessions. Under the agreement made with the radio and telecentre directors, the telecentre staff will continue Internet training and assist in radio browsing production, at least until the presenters become fully competent. The telecentre now plans to budget for digital audio editing software and a minidisk, which will further encourage radio staff to use the centre and to develop radio/telecentre co-productions.

The advantages of a co-production system benefit both parties. The telecentre needs to expand its user-base in order to increase its revenue to the point of being fully sustainable and radio browsing programmes should stimulate demand. Although the radio stations, in return for free services at the centre, had begun broadcasting adverts for the telecentre and its services, it is clear that radio browsing can raise far greater awareness among many more listeners than an advert can.

One of the reasons for low levels of production of development programmes cited by the directors, along with the revenue issue, was the difficulty in getting resource persons to go to the radio stations to take part in programmes. This difficulty should greatly diminish when the resource persons are asked to go to the telecentre to make a programme, as their motivation for going there is far higher: they have email accounts, use Internet and worldprocessing and would generally make good use of a visit. Another benefit for the radios lies in the fact that none of the radio stations previously had a production studio and were only able to make pre-recorded programmes in the few hours per day when they were off air. They now have the option of using the equipment in the telecentre for recorded or live programmes. The telecentre's regular users also represent a reservoir of valuable interviewees.

The telecentre plans to begin producing regular "how to" programmes on ICTs with users as studio guests. The impact on target audiences of a semi-literate Touareg explaining in Tamacheq how he navigates and uses his email is likely to be far higher than if the same explanation is given by a computer engineer. A teenage girl describing in Arabic or Songhai the correspondence she exchanges with email pen friends may, like the nomad, serve as a role model for listeners in her target group.

New programmes are still in the planning stage but a number of existing programmes have been identified as lending themselves to development into browsing programmes. Radio Bouctou has a three-hour programme every evening for the villages of the region and takes calls from relatives abroad with urgent messages, relays announcements and so forth. These villages, which supported the telecentre with donations, have seen little return for their support so far. The director of Radio Bouctou believes that radio browsing for rural audiences could quickly become the first concrete benefit for villagers arising from their investment.

One possibility would be to organise a shared email account for each village, enabling distant relative to send news more often and far less expensively. Browsing programmes could target fishing and farming villages with appropriate information for their economic activities and development needs. Radio Alfarouk uses very young volunteer presenters during the school holidays and these young people could quickly become the "ICT-interface" for school children and students. Not surprisingly, the telecentre has already become a centre of attraction and something of a meeting place for many young people who spend time there every day. Youth browsing programmes could direct them to the best websites for young people and show them that many of their concerns are experienced and discussed by young people all over the world.

The impact of the new telecentre-based radio studio will be monitored for both quantitative and qualitative impact. The number of browsing programmes will be monitored and compared to previous levels of development programming. The number and range of resource persons and the frequency of their participation in browsing programmes will be logged. The topics covered and websites used will be recorded and information on the best web sources made available to all radio staff. Impact will be evaluated in terms of listener response to programmes and request for particular browsing subjects and also in terms of changes in telecentre user patterns. New users will be asked if they decided to come to the centre after following radio browsing programmes and both the number and the range of new users will be matched against radio browsing topics aired.

There are certainly many challenges ahead for the Timbuktu telecentre/radio partnership. There are fewer relevant websites emanating from and intended for developing countries in the French than in the English-speaking world. One response may be to have a focus on CD-ROM browsing as well as Internet browsing. If the telecentre builds up a good library of educational CD-ROMs, for example, this will not only enrich browsing programmes but stimulate demand for use of the computers for learning activities. Another challenge lies in the fact that radio browsing in Timbuktu will have to be done in many more languages than in Kothmale and will have to cater for a far wider range of economic, cultural and social contexts. The radio stations will not derive any direct financial benefit from radio browsing and much will depend on staff motivation. However, indirect financial benefits could include greater support by development partners in response to more effective development programming.

Above all, this is not a new project with a project co-ordinator and it depends on a new dynamic being "spontaneously" created within existing structures: the community telecentre will be seeking to stimulate use of new ICTs by radio stations struggling to compete for very limited advertising revenue.

The most immediate motivation for the radio stations lies in the high potential for raising the quality of their programming and therefore getting a very positive audience response, in the availability within the telecentre of excellent equipment for programme-making and in the readiness of telecentre staff and resource persons to contribute to contents development. In the future, networking is likely to improve the situation for contents development, further easing the problem for the cash-strapped radios of time-consuming development production. Mali's *Maison de la Presse* in Bamako already has a daily on-line radio information service. The telecentre plans to equip each radio station with a modem and a connection to the telecentre as a next step.

The CMC formula adopted in Timbuktu is now being considered as a model in national plans for ICT access in Mali's 703 "communes" or local districts. The plan to build a national network of telecentres, ultimately in every commune, is in the final stages of preparation. An initial target will be to set up telecentres in the 50 main administrative centres of Mali. Originally, planners had decided that the best way to link ICT access with broadcasting would be to equip every radio station (of which Mali has over 100) with a computer and a link to the nearest telecentre. This is now being reconsidered in favour of creating a radio studio within each telecentre for all nearby radio stations to use. First and foremost, this should be more cost-effective in a context where funds for the ambitious national access plan are likely to be hard to come by. Crucially, it will also ensure that radio staff are brought into an ICT–rich environment in which they can benefit fully from training and specialist support. As a first step, this appears preferable to the alternative: introducing minimal ICT equipment into radio studios where there is no specialist back-up to facilitate use of the equipment and where there is no assurance that the equipment will be used adequately.

The contrasting examples of Kothmale and Timbuktu show just how many factors quite extraneous to the actual technology have a determining influence on these two communities' access to new ICTs. In both cases, the goal of *knowledge-sharing* for development is reached through the essential channel of radio broadcasting. It can be argued that individual access to ICTs is also shared in some ways by the individual's circle of family, friends and colleagues. In fact, these two processes together – individual direct access and mass indirect access – offer the optimum formula for achieving both breadth and depth of impact of new ICTs within the community. This is not only because they combine individual empowerment and community empowerment but also because together, they involve the community as a whole in its entry into the knowledge society and knowledge economy.

3

Media and Social Changes

Communication for social change is part of an evolution of communications methodology that can help accelerate global development. The process began in the first quarter of the 20th century with the use of publicity tools to bring attention to social problems such as hunger and disease. It grew to a reliance on public relations as a means of identifying stakeholders and creating programs to fit the audience's interests.

Recently, social marketing took center stage –where sophisticated marketing and cause related advertising tools were applied to influence individual and societal behaviors – such as convincing couples in poor nations to use contraceptives. This was followed by development communications and strategic communications, the latter which rightfully considers communication to be a process rather than as a series of products.

Communication for social change is a distinct way of doing communications – and one of the few approaches that can be sustained. Such sustainability is largely due to the fact that ownership of both the message and the medium – the content and the process – resides with the individuals or communities affected. This approach can help make greater contributions to the pace of development.

Recent developments in communications technologies, in political and media systems, and in emerging development problems suggest a greatly enhanced, radically different role for communication in development programming. Communication programming has, very simplistically, tended to fulfill three roles in development thinking and practice:

First, its role has been to inform and persuade people to adopt certain behaviors and practices that are beneficial to them: for example, to inform people how to protect themselves from HIV and to persuade them to use a condom; to persuade them of the importance of vaccinating their child and to inform them when and where they can do so; to persuade them that simple sugar and salt solutions can cure diarrhea and to inform them how to make them up; to persuade them to have fewer children and to inform them how to do so.

Second, it has been used to enhance the image and profile of the work of organizations involved in development with a view to boosting the credibility of their work, raising more funding and generally improving public perceptions.

Third, it has been used on a more targeted level within communities to enable community consultation over specific initiatives.

The communication for social change initiative believes that all these roles are important and communication work in general remains underfunded and undervalued. These traditional approaches to communication are generally insufficient in addressing the reality of the development problems that exist, and they do not always reflect the complex changes in the communications environments taking place in many developing country societies.

Communication can play a much greater role in enabling people to take control over their own lives, in enabling people and societies to set their own agendas in relation to political, economic and social development; and in enabling, in particular, the voices of the economically and politically marginalized to be amplified and channeled to mainstream public and political debate.

The interaction between communication and the social well-being of people in developing countries will be radically redefined over the next few years. Global economic liberalization of communications, the deployment of the Internet, mobile telephony and other new technologies and the changing political environment in most developing countries are all coinciding to make the cusp of the new millennium a defining moment which will determine how successfully all countries, especially developing nations, adapt to and exploit these changes.

Information in society does not simply enable people to know what they should do or think. Information is power—it enables people to make sense of their lives and it enables them to shape their aspirations. Ultimately it can enable them to take control of their lives. In many areas of the world, people have precious little access to information outside their community that enables them to make such "sense." In other societies, despite a multitude of information outlets, people who are historically marginalized and excluded remain "voiceless" and "invisible" because those who control information channels refuse to share access equitably. Communication for social change principles focus on using direct, many-to-many communications which spring from the affected communities.

The traditional understanding of the role of communication in development is one that seeks mainly to change individual behaviors. This behavior change communication can be broadly defined as a process of understanding people's situations and influences, developing messages that respond to the concerns within those situations, and using communication processes and media to persuade people to increase their knowledge and change the behaviors and practices that place them at risk.

Communication for social change can be defined as a process of public and private dialogue through which people define who they are, what they want and how they can get it. Social change is defined as change in people's lives as they themselves define such change. This work seeks particularly to improve the lives of the politically and economically marginalized, and is informed by principles of tolerance, self-determination, equity, social justice and active participation for all. This approach attempts to rebalance strategic approaches to communication and change by taking the overriding emphasis.

— Away from people as the objects for change and on to people and communities as the agents of their own change

— Away from designing, testing and delivering messages and on to supporting dialogue and debate on the key issues of concern

— Away from the conveying of information from technical experts and on to sensitively placing that information into the dialogue and debate

— Away from a focus on individual behaviors nd on to social norms, policies, culture and a supportive environment

— Away from persuading people to do something and on to negotiating the best way forward in a partnership process

— Away from technical experts in "outside" agencies dominating and guiding the process and on to the people most affected by the issues of concern playing a central role.

Social Change Media

Any reconsideration of social change media must begin from the striking disparity between the programs produced and the needs of the audiences they purport to serve. Funders, producers and critics alike have failed to recognize that social change demands markedly different outcomes from conventional media and hence its own distinct approaches to audience, subject matter and form,

If every social system is, in a sense, the reality of an illusion, then media functions to represent this illusion as reality. During the three decades of Newsreel's existence, the United States has increasingly become a society of consumers rather than citizens, where markets not the civic sector determine more and more social issues. Indeed, many social change activists argue that the nation's most intractable problems result from our reductive definition of social and personal development as economic growth and consumption.

It is logical that in such a society the predominant relationship between the media and its audience should be that of a commodity to its consumer. Film and television aspire to be "eye-grabbing," "spell-binding," or "absorbing" so audiences will both consume and be consumed in their images, thus relieving them of the immemorial phenomenological responsibility of constructing reality for themselves.

Social change media, in contrast, wants to direct its audiences back to their own world; it addresses them not as passive viewers but potentially active participants in civic society. It accordingly recognizes that its true subject is always the audience itself, specifically, how that audience is constructing social reality in their minds and daily lives. It locates itself not in the narrative space of the television or movie screen but as an intervention in society's continuing self-narrating around and beyond those screens.

Like a skilled conversationalist, social change media aims to integrate itself into this discourse, raising questions, reframing arguments, suggesting new directions or additional resources, in short, providing a structuring frame for these larger civic sector conversations. As social change media texts become more integrated into their context, that context, social life, will become more "textualized," more articulated and problematized, as a subject for democratic discussion.

Social change media therefore is committed not to its own self-expression but to faciliataing the discourse of communities joined around social change. It does not, however, define these communities as market niches or demographic groups as a commercial cable network like Univision, MTV or Lifetime might. It also rejects any essentialist or traditionalist view of community as unified primarily around historical differences from a dominant culture. Instead, social change communities are joined around a systemic critique of the status quo and committed to developing a more inclusive social vision.

In the familiar formulation, they are communities not just in themselves but for themselves, more concerned about what they can become than what they have been. Cornel West and Sylvia Ann Hewlett, for example, have recently suggested forming a movement cutting across race, class and gender lines around the revitalization of parenting and one can imagine similar deliberately transformative communities coalescing around other core social activities.

The long-term development of such discursive communities, however, cannot be advanced by the short-term, program-centered funding presently favored by most foundations and television networks. The waste of such project-based funding can be graphically illustrated by the Independent Television Service (ITVS), currently the largest funder of social change media in the country. Created by Congress in 1988 after lobbying by independent producers, ITVS has distributed over $60,000,000 for hundreds of one-off programs and series, broadcast desultorily across the PBS schedule.

Because ITVS has defined its primary mandate as funding independent productions, it has missed the chance to create coherent, sustained blocks of public service programming which might be capable of attracting new, under-served audiences to public television and of nurturing the growth of social change communities. ITVS actually retreated from just such an opportunity. A group of independent producers from Chicago proposed a weekly magazine program, Grassroots Journal, conceived as a public television "how-to" show, not for gardeners, cooks or investors, but neighborhood activists. It was designed to offer a high-visibility national gateway to a field which, like so many areas of social change, is fragmented into numerous, under-funded, local organizations.

The Benton Foundation even created an interactive, internet-based "Grassroots Toolbox" to accompany the series containing resources and hot-links back to activist organizations in viewers' local communities. The program was to be broadcast and heavily promoted across the widening spectrum of potential outlets for social change programs: public television stations (especially overlap signals,) PEG channels and frequencies opened up by digital compression. Two pilots were actually produced with the support of ITVS and an informal network of inner city public television stations. ITVS, however, dropped the project on the usual nebulous grounds that it wasn't "good television" but it hasn't attempted any similar public service series since.

A program from post-apartheid South Africa demonstrates that such projects are not hopelessly Utopian and that with commitment and imagination media can be effectively integrated into larger social change strategies. The Soul City multi-media project is organized around a weekly television drama, scripted collaboratively by professional screenwriters and public health professionals. Try to imagine ER or General Hospital set in a Soweto clinic with continuing story lines around AIDS awareness, quitting smoking and child abuse. This television series is coordinated with radio programs broadcast in eight languages, feature columns in daily papers and popular comic books distributed in doctors' offices and community centers.

Now in its third season, Soul City is reputedly South Africa's most popular domestically produced program and has been widely hailed as a path-breaking innovation in public health education. The best they seem to have been able to achieve are expensive, prestigious prime time series with accompanying coffee table books eulogizing social change movements while embalming them in celluloid. Apart from children's programming, there is not a single continuing strand of non-commercial public service media currently in production on film or television - nothing about aging, working life, inner city renewal, alternative education, immigrant life or media reform.

Many trust that new interactive, internet-based technologies will create these public service media environments but, while technical innovation will undoubtedly play a role, we should not be seduced by technological determinism. Four times already in this century new communications technologies - film, radio, broadcast television and cable - have been introduced with "Blue Sky" promises of a rebirth of civic society. And each time they have been used for the same meretricious commercial purposes; the quantity not the quality of media choices has increased. The task confronting media activists is to integrate existing and future technical resources into effective communications infrastructures for specific social change communities so we can revitalize our enervated civic sphere.

As a precondition to becoming useful partners in social change organizing, producers and funders must give up their present media-centered perspective for an audience-centered one; they must come to think of their audience not as viewers but users of media. Since these twelve points suggest a substantial shift in how we produce and fund media, they probably should be regarded as just a first tentative step towards putting the social change back into social change media.

1. Funders should support social change media projects only if they are designed as part of coherent, long-term strategies for community building centered in the work of existing organizations.

2. Funders must free themselves from project-based grantmaking and commit themselves to long-term support for the development of specific, alternative discourses on social policy. For example, they should favor on-going blocks of programming, journals nationwide op-ed and advertizing campaigns and combinations of these rather than one-off programs or series.

3. Funders must not be afraid to make media grants directly to educational and activist organizations, not just filmmakers and television networks.

4. Any responsible social change media grantmaking must be based on rigorous assessment of the media needs of particular areas of social change organizing. Reliable ascertainment and evaluation tools for social change media need to be developed.

5. Social change activists will usually not have the media expertise or inclination to translate their organizing needs into innovative and effective media solutions. Analogously, media activists do not have the hands-on organizing experience or strategic perspective to identify those needs.

6. Therefore funders will have to set up incubators or workshops drawing together potential, community-based media users to specify their needs and then to work with media professionals to articulate appropriate media responses.
7. Funders may also want to sponsor internship or residency programs pairing media professionals with social change organizations so media makers can learn about their daily operations and then suggest appropriate media systems and programming.
8. While there will no doubt still be a place for conventional "linear" documentary, grantmakers may have to develop a new cadre of social change media producers skilled in working collaboratively with organizers and in designing multi-media solutions to their problems.
9. TThe definition of social change media must be expanded beyond films and television programs to include PSA and billboard campaigns, short discussion starters, internet chat rooms and web-sites, even cable channels devoted to particular areas of social change.
10. Projects must justify their choice of technology as the most appropriate and cost-effective for their specific objectives rather than be driven by technological glitz or Hollywood glamour.
11. Over time, as new technologies are implemented, social change media may tend to resemble an interactive infrastructure more than discrete texts.
12. This frankly utilitarian production strategy may preclude the occasional masterpiece but it should immeasurably lift the overall accountability and cost-effectiveness of social change media.

Media produced within these parameters can play a strategic role in social change because it represents, or rather presents, society as something already under discussion, in the here and now, by media users, joined into transformative communities. In other words, it provides a communications infrastructure for the revolution of everyday life; it conceives democracy not just as a competition between large special interests but as a laboratory for social innovation at a grassroots level. Such a social change media can serve as a frame and forum for the exfoliation of alternative civic discourses, communities and social movements. But this will only happen if the funders, producers and distributors of social change media are willing to abandon their present text-based approach for a context-based one, not substituting for civic conversations but facilitating them. In these chiliastic times when many claim politics has reached an end, it is at least a beginning to create the spaces where more can be said.

Current Trends in Communications Environment

The "communications environment" in which most people on the planet live has changed radically over the last decade. It has changed both in relation to the information people have access to, and the opportunities people have to communicate their own perspectives on issues that concern them. This new communications environment is shaped by three main interlocking trends:

1. Media liberalization and deregulation
2. New information and communication technologies
3. The changing global political and economic context

In general, and with important exceptions, these trends are tending to decentralize communications in developing countries, with a trend towards a more fragmented, more horizontal, people-to-people model of communication, and away from a highly centralized, vertical model. In industrialized countries, media liberalization suggests more choice for consumers, which should, theoretically, mean increased access. Yet the way it plays out in countries like the United States is in encouraging the growth of huge media monopolies that result in far less community input to programming. With deregulation, public service programming has become just a fading memory, and station ownership has leaped beyond the realm of possibility for most community-based organizations or individuals of color.

This new communications environment has, we argue, important implications for development programming, an importance that is compounded by the emergence of new development problems—such as HIV/AIDS—that demand new approaches to communication. There are many opportunities to be seized, as well as real challenges to be faced in understanding and acting upon these changes.

Media Liberalization

Most people on this planet receive most of their information on issues beyond their immediate communities from the print and broadcast media. Fifteen years ago, much of humanity had one main source for this information—their governments. The means were stolid, formulaic broadcast and print media that had been established with the express purpose of telling people what they should know and think. Two general trends have changed this.

First, following the end of the Cold War, a combination of internal pressure from their citizens and external pressure—often in the form of conditions set by donors—have led governments to relax censorship and freedom of speech laws.

Second, this pressure for political liberalization has been combined with economic liberalization and deregulation of national media industries.

The result in many of those countries with tightly controlled media has been a blossoming of dynamic, generally populist and highly commercial newspapers, television and radio media in most developing countries, and flourishing of new community media in some. Meanwhile, old monopoly state-run media, particularly broadcasters, have tended to languish, losing their audiences to more dynamic competition. They also face declining government support and funding.

The implications of these changes for those involved in communication are challenging. Monopoly broadcasters have presented a convenient way of communicating simple messages to huge audiences through one medium. In much more fragmented media environments, this opportunity no longer exists and reaching the same audience requires putting messages out through many different media, and adapting it to many different audiences.

Perhaps more importantly, the creation of these more complex and dynamic communications environments raises the deeper question of just what information do people have access to, and does it empower poor people and give them a greater voice—or does it move them further to the economic and social margins? At their worse, new communications environments have done the latter. They have shifted from providing stodgy and dogmatic government propaganda to providing a uniform diet of often Western popular music.

In some countries, state-controlled news has been replaced by no news, or information that is sensational, inaccurate or irrelevant to the daily lives of much of its audience, or news that is derived entirely from international sources. Often operating in anarchic regulatory environments, commercial and private stations have little obligation to provide anything other than entertainment. At its very worst, media have encouraged intolerance, sectionalism and tribalism, the most extreme example being the "hate" radio of RTML in Rwanda which played a key role in the massacres in that country.

At their best, however, commercial, community and, in some cases, newly invigorated state-run news and media organizations have managed to attract large audiences with compelling, popular and informative programming. In Kampala, Uganda, the FM station Capital Radio attracts some of its highest audiences for its Capital Doctor program, which provides advice and information on issues of sex, HIV/AIDS and other health issues. In South Africa, a form of "edutainment" –"Soul City," set in a Johannesburg township—has become one of the most popular soap operas in the country, yet has succeeded in educating people about diarrhea, HIV/AIDS and other issues.

Again in South Africa, deregulation has spurred the creation of more than 80 community radio stations broadcasting in 15 languages. Community stations have made serious inroads into the broadcast markets, often stealing audiences from the well-established public broadcasting stations. Community broadcasting provides communities with information that is relevant to their lives, as well as a voice through which people can make demands. In Cape Town, the tiny community radio station, Radio Zibonele, drew on their audience's anger to play a key role in mediating and resolving the township's gang warfare surrounding the taxi business. In fact, the success of community radio proves, in some small way, the ready market for communication for social change principles to be applied in diverse circumstances throughout the world. In addition to sub-Saharan African nations, community radio has succeeded where little else can from northwest Canada to southeast Asia.

The print media too is changing under similar pressure, with more entertaining, more populist and often more trenchant coverage of news issues. These changes have demonstrated how in the print media in particular, poor reporting undermines many other forms of social and political discourse; high quality reporting can play a major role in promoting and stimulating constructive public debate. Well-informed, investigative reporting in particular can provide a key element of public accountability, both for national governments, for international institutions, and for NGOs and other civil society organizations.

The last decade has seen an explosion in satellite broadcasting. Take the South Asia region, home to one-fifth of the world's population which is today within the footprint of at least 50 broadcast satellites. In India, Pakistan and Bangladesh alone there are more than 70 million households with television sets, adding up to a total viewership of 300 million. By 2007, there will be 550 million television viewers in these countries. Half of them will be hooked up to cable – able to watch the 350 channels that will be available to them by then. These changes do not apply to all people in all countries, but in one form or another they do affect the vast majority of people in the great majority of countries. They present many problems; reaching lots of people with prepared messages is becoming more difficult and more expensive. They also present substantial opportunities: to work with communities to enable them to amplify their voices, to enable access to the information that can empower them, to help shape communication environments that can work for people, not against them.

Revolution of ICTs

The current revolution in information communications technologies (ICTs) represents probably the most profound set of technological developments human society has experienced since the industrial revolution. The innovations of the Internet—and particularly e-mail—have transformed communications capacities in countries with often dilapidated telecommunications infrastructures; and have opened up access to much more information about global issues.

The falling costs and increased access to telephony mean that an increasing number of people have the capacity to communicate rapidly beyond their immediate communities, thus opening up new economic opportunities and opportunities for social and political discourse. For many participants in this communication for social change initiative these technologies represent a huge opportunity:

— Centralized control of information by governments or commercial interests becomes much more difficult. Increasingly, political systems can neither control the information their citizens receive nor monitor or constrain how they communicate with each other. Technology is—for good and ill—increasing access to the kind of information that is uncensored and unfiltered. Technology is growing most rapidly in those areas where its demand is most clearly defined by the users.

— The capacity of people to access information is substantially increased.

— The capacity of people to organize, advocate and lobby beyond physical boundaries is greatly enhanced.

— The capacity for people and organizations in developing countries to communicate information—their aspirations, demands, experiences, analysis—becomes cheaper, more powerful and far more pervasive.

Nevertheless, we also recognize the limitations of these technologies. In particular, the "information gap" between rich and poor is stark. One of the least expensive of the information and communications technologies (ICTs) — the telephone—illustrates just how far apart the rich and poor worlds are in access to such technologies. One quarter of the countries in the world still have fewer than one telephone line per 100 people.

The majority of the population in developing countries — 60% of the total—live in rural areas. Yet in these countries, more than 80% of main telephone lines are in urban areas. The distribution of new ICTs is no more equal. Eighty four per cent of mobile cellular subscribers,

91% of all fax machines and 97% of Internet host computers are in developed countries.

Telecommunications is nevertheless becoming cheaper, more reliable and more accessible and will continue to do so. Despite the constraints, it seems likely that we are seeing the emergence internationally of organizational structures that are increasingly based on networks, rather than hierarchies. It is this revolution which represents most powerfully the increase in horizontal, people-to-people communication, and which provides profound new opportunities for more inclusive public and policy debate.

Changing Political and Economic Environment

The collapse of the Soviet Union and the end of the Cold War have had far reaching effects, a full exploration of which is beyond the remit of this chapter. However, two key issues should be mentioned. The first is the growing, though uneven, democratization and political liberalization that has swept much of the developing world over the last decade. Many of the highly centralized oneparty states or dictatorships have given way to multi-party democracies, or at least to more open political systems. This political liberalization has been matched by a still more pervasive economic liberalization and we have seen the rapid emergence of a new global economy.

As Manuel Castells argues, "for the first time in human history the entire planet is capitalist, since even the few remaining command economies are surviving or developing through their linkages to global, capitalist markets." As all governments are finding, including China's, maintaining strict and centralized control of information in a market economy is both difficult and often inefficient.

The fragmentation and decentralization of information outlined above is potentially countered by the greater concentration of ownership in communications and media industries ushered in by globalization. According to UNESCO's World Communication Report 1997, "international [media] conglomerates are emerging with the purpose of controlling not only the transmission system (manufacturing, network, cable, satellite etc.) but also the programs they convey."

An increasing spate of mergers and acquisitions over recent years has seen the emergence of a handful of "world companies" who now dominate global media markets. Time Warner Inc., News International, Sony, Finivest and Bertelsman each have annual sales well in excess of $10 billion, an increasing percentage of which is generated outside the United States. This concentration is compounded by convergence of media and telecommunications industries leading to still greater concentration of ownership.

Such concentration may not matter and may be offset by the more horizontal and decentralized models of communications. But both these trends—towards a decentralization of information production away from government, and a concentration of ownership of the means of communication in the hands of transnationals—should matter to anyone involved in communication. These trends are bound up intimately with questions of who controls the information that people receive.

Emerging Development Problems

These changes to communication environments come at the same time as important changes in how we think about development. Some of the most important emerging development challenges of the last decade have raised new questions. Issues such as HIV/AIDS, reproductive health and reproductive rights, and others such as tobacco use have highlighted more intensely than ever how disease and poor health are linked not only to poverty and poor nutrition, but also to prejudice, to social, political and economic inequality, and to social dislocation. They have focused an especially strong spotlight on social and political environments where issues of sex and sexuality are habitually hidden or are difficult to debate in public.Such complexities are forcing societies globally to change—to question long cherished, deeply rooted social, political, and religious mores and practices. A whole range of issues—from HIV to reproductive rights, from domestic violence to female genital mutilation—have crystallized the need for much wider social and political change. Such change is informed by what happens both within countries and by international debates, but if it is to be sustainable, change has to emerge from within societies.

The means of how societies change, and who drives such change is contentious and difficult. Part of such change will come from education about issues such as condom use—but much of the more deep seated changes that need to take place in societies, such as the improvement in the status of women, need to emerge from advocacy and vigorous public debate within and between societies. Such debates depend fundamentally on communication: on communication within societies, within families, within communities, through political discourse;

and on communication between societies, at the levels of the individual, of the community and of the global society. The capacity of people to communicate is intimately bound up with their capacity to effect change. In short, a new model of communication could be emerging from a mixture of political, technological, economic and social change. It is decentralized, pluralistic and democratic; it seeks to empower rather than persuade people; it fosters debate among and between citizens, among and between communities, and between people and government. This model envisages increasingly horizontal communication allowing people to communicate with each other easily and inexpensively. It also involves the steady disintegration of traditional monolithic vertical lines of communication, where governments owned radio and television stations in order to control flows of information.

Creating an Environment for Change

The role of communication in developing country societies is changing, and that the strategies of those working in development needed to change with it. The changes that are taking place in communication and society may have profound implications for donor and development strategies, but that this premise remains poorly researched and articulated.

Communication for social change programming suggests a major shift in development. Above all it is about enabling publics and communities to articulate their own agendas for development — at the community, the provincial, the national and the international level. Programming in this area is about making connections— at these different levels and between them. It involves making connections between global trade policies and local communities, and it involves making connections between many different kinds of activities—between the issues themselves and the means that exist for debating and discussing them: community radio, women's radio listeners groups, an informed and responsive national media, quality media programming, telecommunications.

It involves framing and phrasing debates in language and forms that are inclusive. It involves a responsibility of academics in particular, but those concerned with development in general, to communicate research and information not only to their peers, but to the wider public within developing countries. It involves "returning" research and analysis to where it originates. It suggests that the key role for donor and development institutions is to create an environment for change.

It also suggests a role that sees these organizations continuing to inform and create development strategies, but also in creating the conditions where developing country societies can assess, challenge and adapt such strategies and begin to create strategies for themselves. It provides new opportunities to open up development decisions and programming to public debate and dialogue, and to enable publics—and not just experts—to be more proactive in shaping debate on development issues.

The current communications efforts to promote an enhanced discipline known as communication for social change grows. Today most progressive U.S.-based foundations are in the business of positive social change –change in attitudes, in behaviors, in utilization of technology, and of access to opportunities to enhance lives. Being key players in the development arena, these foundations' focus remain predominantly on science-based knowledge. Yet at the core of much of these foundations'current portfolio is the need to affect individual and community norms and behaviors – the type of change that requires sophisticated, sustained communication.

The most likely practitioners of communication for social change are small struggling organizations with few resources. Communication for social change in some respects becomes a means of survival. Without the benefit of large communications staffs or budgets, and facing media that are hesitant to cover social issues in substantive ways, some small NGOs and community-based organizations have figured out how to use the people most affected by their work to make the communications process work.

In Africa and Latin America, the community radio movement stands out. By definition, community radio stations cannot succeed without local control, citizen participation, local issuesbased programming and open access. Yet radio remains essentially a top-down methodology; that is, someone decides what will be broadcast, it airs, and is received passively by listeners. The better community radio stations, such as Cape Flats' Bush Radio, Radio Zibonele in the Khayelitsha community of Cape Town, South Africa, and Alexandra Township's community station focus on audience participation. New programming stems from the suggestions listeners make when phoning into the stations, or when they are working there as volunteer staff.

Recognition of the role of communication in achieving social change is not necessarily new nor surprising, but it receives comparatively little funding. While the case for this kind of programming—for the reasons already given—

is building, there remain significant obstacles to it attracting major support.

Many of the communications initiatives that are currently funded—particularly around behavior change—attract support less because they are perceived as addressing the main problem, but more because they can be claimed as having changed something. In the field of HIV/AIDS, for example, much of the funding for communications initiatives has gone into attempts to change individual behaviors.

Communication for social change programming can constitute only part of the real solution; it can help enable people to shape their own agenda, articulate their own priorities and aspirations of how to address the epidemic, and ensure that donors are following and responding to public and policy debates within developing countries as well as shaping such debates. Evaluation of impact in this area remains difficult but not, we conclude, impossible. It does, however, mean that we must develop new methodologies.

Donors have a right and an obligation to demand evidence that their funds have been spent wisely, that they have achieved what they were meant to, or that there are good reasons for any changes or lack of achievement. However, there are other reasons why impact needs to be measured.

1. *Accountability* – understanding the impact of communication interventions is an essential component of being accountable. The primary accountability is to the people engaged in the communication intervention. Being involved with them in aspects of their lives requires that

accountability. They are also the people, proportionate to their means, who will invest the most resources.

2. *Progress* – understanding what is happening and whether it is what people want to happen.
3. *Improvement* – information from any measurement and evaluation is crucial to both large strategic decisions and to fine tuning communication interventions in order that better value is gained from the investments that are made.
4. *Motivation* – a sense of achievement is crucial to motivation. Good motivation is an essential element of any endeavor, including communication for social change programs. The people involved draw energy and drive from knowing that progress is being made. Not knowing can lead to the opposite.
5. *Credibility* – Good data on the impact of communication for social change interventions can only enhance the credibility of this field and the investments – from local to international –that are made.

The long-term goal of all development action is to see positive change in the issues of concern. We all want less poverty, increased employment, better gender equality, to eradicate HIV/AIDS, more girls in school, higher educational achievement, lower child and maternal mortality rates, better nutrition, fewer accidents and no violence. That is the crucial measure of success. Such changes can take five years or a decade, but generally much longer.

People involved in communication for social change initiatives need more immediate data that indicates whether what they are doing is making a contribution to the overall change process. It is not possible to run a program for 15 years before assessing impact and then finding that the wrong things were done. More immediate information on the contribution of communication to change is required.

Although communication for social change activities tend to have less specific and immediate objectives and targets, they nevertheless need to develop a similar set of indicators both to measure and indicate progress and to drive the nature of the programming.

Some suggestions of indicators include:

— *Expanded public and private dialogue and debate*: Dialogue and debate are crucial. They indicate that people are engaging in the issues of concern, are motivated to look at them, and that at least some of the parties to the debate and discussion are challenging the orthodoxy that may be contributing to the matters of most concern. For example, the role of women in politics; the need for a more open approach to sexual health issues; equal rights for boys and girls; and land redistribution.

— *Increased accuracy of the information that people share in the dialogue/debate*: Accuracy of information is important. There are two types of information. First where there is specific, proven data such as would exist in relation to a particular medical issue. Second, accurately reflecting the background information, perspectives and views of the parties to a debate over a more complex issue such as girls in school. The more accurately the data and the perspectives are reflected in the dialogue – from among friends to public policy debate – the more likely is the chance of positive change.

— The means available that enable people/communities to feed their voices into debate and dialogue.

— *Increased leadership and agenda setting role by disadvantaged people on the issues of concern:* Whatever the focus of the communication for social change action the people at the center of the issues – those whose everyday lives are most affected – should be involved in the major decisions related to the initiative. This will ensure relevance and meaning – a vital component for any intervention.

— *Resonates with the major issues of interest to people's everyday interests:* Communication for social change interventions need to be positioned in ways that resonate, make sense to them, to which they can relate. Of course this is a basic tenet of all communication, but it can be easily forgotten in the midst of complex detail relating to an issue such as breast feeding and HIV/AIDS. If the positioning of the issue does resonate there is a greater chance of momentum and action. And it is not possible to focus on all the many and varied aspects of a concern. Rarely can the issue that resonates be chosen in advance. It will emerge and then needs to be accentuated.

— *Linked people and groups with similar interests who might otherwise not be in contact:* One of the main turning points for any change process is when different groups form alliances with a common overall objective and a loose coordination framework. Each group does its own thing, but in the knowledge that it contributes to a greater effort. Therefore activities that link people together and help working alliances can be interpreted as contributing to positive change.

Throughout the NGO community in industrialized and in less wealthy nations, the potential both to apply communication for social change methodology and to encourage its use is great. The change communication principles seem obvious to those in development, philanthropy and social services. They speak to the very essence of the work – that is, to helping create locallybased solutions to critical social ills. The strategy for moving this initiative forward has five prongs:

1. Reaching clarity of terms and defining, or perhaps refining, the field;
2. Identifying and describing the skills, attributes and resources necessary for communication for social change. During the Cape Town conference, participants discussed both the form and content of the skills development process.
3. Developing the systems and exchange mechanisms needed to spread the change communication work globally;
4. Maintaining the network of supporters and enrolling others; and,
5. Using concrete measurements to evaluate effectiveness and the reach of communication for social change.

Communication Strategies to Control HIV/AIDS

The HIV/AIDS pandemic arguably presents the starkest, gravest, most complex development challenge the development communication community has ever faced. While important advances have been made in the effort to contain HIV, the reality behind this meeting is that more than 36 million people are now HIV+ and up to one in four of the adult population of the most heavily affected countries now carry the virus. Conversely, there is also greater optimism, energy and commitment surrounding the epidemic than there has been for many years.

HIV/AIDS has over the last two years become the focus of more intense international attention than any other public health issue facing the developing world, a process which culminated at the UN General Assembly Special Session on AIDS (UNGASS) in June this year and the establishment of a new global fund. After years of conferences, lobbying by international agencies and civil society organisations, and the growing evidence of the scale of the crisis, 2001 saw the potential turning point where the international community made HIV/AIDS a major international priority.

In the late 1980s there was a similar upsurge of international policy and public debate on HIV/AIDS with donors increasing their funding to tackle the epidemic and with intensive international media coverage focused on the issue. This international attention waned in the 1990s, partly because the epidemic did not materialise as a significant problem in the North, partly because of the decline in political advocacy in the North around the epidemic once antiretroviral treatments became more widely available, and partly because of the complexity of the epidemic and the lack of short term gains.

In the last few years, however, two issues have brought HIV/AIDS firmly back on to development agendas. The first is the (re)recognition of the scale of the epidemic itself. The second is the development of combination therapy of antiretroviral drugs, which quickly became widely available in the North, but unavailable to most people living with HIV/AIDS. This issue became the catalyst and focal point for arguably the first genuinely southern driven global movement in response to the epidemic.

The efforts of individuals and organisations to bring HIV/AIDS back onto the agenda of Northern governments paid fruit in 2000, when the G8 group of nations discussed the issue at the Okinaw a summit. That meeting, combined with many other initiatives brought about the process that led to UNGASS in June 2001 - the first time that such a session had been called to discuss a health issue - and the establishment of the Global Health Fund in the same year.

The Declaration of Commitment on HIV/AIDS that emerged from UNGASS was subject to intense and prolonged debate during its drafting, with some of the language, particularly on groups most at risk, being watered down. Nonetheless, it remains a stronger document than some critics had feared and, if applied, a potentially powerful tool mandating governments and others to undertake a wide range of actions. These include the development of "national strategies and financing plans for combating HIV/AIDS that address the epidemic in forthright terms" and to "confront stigma, silence and denial; address gender and age-based dimensions of the epidemic; eliminate discrimination and marginalization."

Furthermore, actors are urged to "involve partnerships with civil society and the business sector and the full participation of people living with HIV/AIDS, those in vulnerable groups and people mostly at risk, particularly women and young people ... fully promote and protect all human rights and fundamental freedoms, including the right to the highest attainable standard of physical and mental health."

Nowthat the epidemic is once again on the international agenda, the hope is that this time, compared to the 1980s and 1990s, commitments made will be met. However, it remains to be seen how effective the Declaration will be. Many observers doubt that the deadlines and evaluation mechanisms it imposes for developing strategies will be met by many countries. Nonetheless, they believe that the language in the Declaration will provide a tool for NGOs and others to pressure their governments to take appropriate action and the Declaration will prove itself over time as the concepts it describes are incorporated into other documents and the general discourse on HIV/AIDS and development.

The biggest question marks hang over the newly created Global Fund. There remain a number of areas of uncertainty over the likely impact of the Fund; there are major concerns as to whether the fund will actually lead to new money being made available: there is continuing uncertainty as to the differing emphases on prevention and treatment; there are concerns over how the funds will be channelled, and particular concerns over representation on involvement in setting spending priorities for the fund.

Nevertheless, there is a demonstrable new energy and commitment around HIV/AIDS from the international community, with new funding not only being channelled into the new Fund but also from existing and major new donors in this field. One of the challenges facing the Communication for Development Roundtable is identifying the most effective strategies on which this still inadequate resource based can be used.

The last two years have seen intense debate over different approaches to HIV/AIDS communication. In particular, there has been a growing questioning of social marketing and behaviour change oriented communication, and increased interest and debate focused in the field of Communication for Social Change, an approach to communication that focuses less on changing individual behaviours and more on empowering communities and societies to tackle the underlying issues of discrimination, poverty and marginalisation that are driving the epidemic in the first place. As these issues are closely related to the substance of the Roundtable, this section seeks to explain some of the main issues involved.

Two developments in particular have focused debate on this area, the first the publication of a new framework on Communication produced by UNAIDS, the second the work of the Rockefeller Foundation in this area.

UNAIDS New Communication Framework

This UNAIDS framework was published in December 1999 following an intensive process of detailed consultations in Asia, Africa, Latin America and the Caribbean and internationally. Its conclusions were that:

"Based on a review of the literature and of experiences in the field, most current theories and models [of HIV communication programming] did not provide an adequate foundation on which to develop communications interventions for HIV/AIDS in the regions... Participants at five consultative workshops (two global and three regional) noted the inadequacy and limitations of current theories and the models derived from them. Chief among the weaknesses identified were:

— The simple, linear relationship between individual knowledge and action, which underpinned many earlier interventions, does not take into account the variation among the political, socio-economic and cultural contexts that prevail in the regions.

— External decision-making processes that cater to rigid, narrow ly focused and short term interests tend to overlook the benefits of long-term, internally derived, broad-based solutions.

— There is an assumption that decisions about HIV/AIDS prevention are based on rational, volitional thinking with no regard for more true-to-life emotional responses to engaging in sexual behaviour.

— There is an assumption that creating aw areness through media campaigns will necessarily lead to behaviour change.

— There is an assumption that a simple strategy designed to trigger a once in a lifetime behaviour, such as immunization, would be adequate for changing and maintaining complex, life-long behaviours, such as consistent condom use.

— There is a nearly exclusive focus on condom promotion to the exclusion of the need to address the importance and centrality of social contexts, including government policy, socio-economic status, culture, gender relations and spirituality.

— Approaches based on traditional family planning and population program strategies tend to target HIV/AIDS prevention to women, so that women, rather than men, are encouraged to initiate the use of condoms."

The UNAIDS framework made a series of recommendations and set out a new framework for HIV/AIDS prevention. The conclusions of the framework were summarised very effectively in a paper prepared for UNAIDS by Arvind Singhal:

> "The UNAIDS framework calls for refocusing communication interventions on the basis of five key contextual domains: (1) government policy, (2) socioeconomic status, (3) culture, (4) gender relations, and (5) spirituality. These contextual domains, while they lie outside the control of individuals, have a significant influence on their HIV/AIDS-related health behaviours. In essence, the UNAIDS framework calls for moving away from individual-level theories and models of preventive health behaviours (health belief models, theory of reasoned action, stages of change, hierarchy of effects model, social cognitive theory, diffusion of innovations, and others) to more multilevel, cultural, and contextual explanations and interventions."

While mass education campaigns aimed at changing individual behaviour play an essential role in AIDS prevention, they are highly unlikely to be successful or sustainable unless they are accompanied by deep-rooted social changes which will only result from internally driven change processes, including informed and inclusive public debate.

Many millions of dollars have been spent on individually targeted education campaigns, and many of these campaigns have had important impacts. Increasingly, how ever, concern is mounting that these campaigns are at best insufficient in achieving the kind of long term, sustainable and rooted changes in society that are required for HIV/AIDS to be confronted.

The principles and approach associated with *Communication for Social Change* have been summarised as moving communication frameworks on HIV/AIDS...

— "away from people as the objects for change ... and on to people and communities as the agents of their own change

— away from designing, testing and delivering messages ... and on to supporting dialogue and debate on the key issues of concern

— away from the conveying of information from technical experts ... and on to sensitively placing that information into the dialogue and debate

— away from a focus on individual behaviours ... and on to social norms, policies, culture and a supportive environment

— away from persuading people to do something ... and on to negotiating the best way forw ard in a partnership process

— away from technical experts in "outside" agencies dominating and guiding the process ... and on to the people most affected by the issues of concern playing a central role".

The chief criticism levelled at these arguments in particular, and Communication for Social Change (CSC) advocates in general, is that they are saying little that is new. Specific criticisms tend to fall into four areas.

First, that participatory, people centred communication has been at the core of most mainstream communication thinking and practice for many years, and most development communication initiatives aim first and foremost to empow er people to make informed choices. In this context, argue the critics, much of what CSC proponents are arguing is a reiteration of much of what has gone before.

Second, that some of these arguments are creating artificial boundaries between different approaches and schools of thought in communication. Good communication interventions focus on an intelligent and locally appropriate mix of behaviour change, social change, advocacy and other forms of communication. In focusing on moving away from "traditional" approaches to communication, CSC proponents are creating an unnecessary tension between different approaches to communication when what is needed is a synthesis between a range of interventions.

Third, that while the UNAIDS arguments have emerged largely from practitioners on the ground, and while there is along academic tradition of participatory communication literature, CSC arguments are weak when it comes to backing their arguments up with rigorous academic analysis, modelling and theory. Similarly, they are weak in providing effective evaluation methodologies which can demonstrate the impact of their work.

Fourth, that while many of the ideas in documents such as the UNAIDS Communication Framework are strong in terms of principle, they are difficult to translate into practice on the ground, particularly within the setting of large institutions.

Proponents of Communication for Social Change acknowledge some of these criticisms. Nevertheless, they argue, while there is a rich and mainstream tradition of participatory communication, particularly in the field of HIV/AIDS this is not being applied. They point to a number of factors in response to criticisms made of them.

First, that both the UNAIDS and Rockefeller processes were centred on largely southern based, grassroots and civil society focused and driven debates. These processes appear to have revealed widespread perceptions on the ground that HIV/AIDS communication initiatives in developing countries' are significantly driven by institutional and external agencies operating according to their own assessment of what needs to be done, rather than supporting and working within a framework of genuinely internally driven debates and agendas around HIV/AIDS. In this sense, they appear to have revealed a substantial "disconnect" between funding and some international agencies, and indigenous organisations working on the ground. Such organisations, these processes suggest, perceive that 'mainstream communication interventions are often highly vertical, and are constructed through a process through which they feel they are sometimes partners, and in which they are sometimes involved, but over which they feel they have little control.

Second, that while participatory communication is indeed mainstream thinking among communication theorists and practitioners, systematically putting these principles into practice on the ground continues to be extremely difficult. Participatory and social change communications tends to work on long time horizons, to be difficult to evaluate in terms of impact and difficult for donors to support. For these reasons, most financial support tends to be channelled to interventions, such as social marketing programmes, with short time horizons, and with clear and quantitative evaluation mechanisms. Many proponents of Communication for Social Change argue that these channels of communications are generally marginal and peripheral add ons to otherw ise vertical and behaviour change oriented programmes, while they should provide the core and foundation of all other interventions.

Third, that in challenging the perceived emphasis on behaviour change interventions, it is not intended to create a false dichotomy between the various different approaches, but there is a strong argument that unless developing country societies and communities are setting and driving the underlying processes of change that are necessary to confront this epidemic, and unless support is provided for the creation of environments where that can happen, future progress in tackling HIV/AIDS is unlikely to be sustainable. They argue that developing countries, both in terms of government and civil society, still find themselves in a position where they are responding to rather than shaping the international response to HIV/AIDS.

Fourth, that while theory and academic rigour are weak points in terms of Communication for Social Change interventions, there is increasing interest in learning from and adapting the rigorous thinking that goes into much behaviour change oriented interventions to communication for social change thinking.

Fifth, they argue that Communication for Social Change, while poorly defined, is not only suggesting the incorporation of more participatory techniques in existing project programming, but a major change in approach which involves institutions surrendering their agendas.

Sixth, they argue that many communication initiatives are overly focused on the symptoms of the HIV/AIDS pandemic, rather than the underlying causes. While high rates of sexual transmission are undeniably the principal driver for rapid spread of the virus, and changing sexual behaviour is necessary to contain the pandemic, behaviour change is unlikely to be achieved without addressing the underlying causes of these behaviours. Issues of inequality, prejudice, the status of women, the responsibility of men, marginalisation and disempow erment, community and social cohesion, poverty and many other social and political factors are fundamental drivers of the pandemic. Addressing these issues is also fundamentally about using and fostering communications in society.

And finally, they argue that the dispute is not necessarily an either/or issue and that clearly there is huge value in many behaviour change and social marketing interventions. Nevertheless, they argue that unless these are implemented within a broader social and political context then there are major limitations in terms of sustainability and impact.

The last two years have also seen, arguably, a major change in the dynamics of the debate over HIV.Since the beginning of the epidemic in the mid 1980s, civil society and AIDS support organisations in developing countries have struggled to make their voice heard internationally. While their North American and European civil society counterparts in the North, principally in the gay movement, formed extremely effective and highly organised caucuses to place the issues of HIV/AIDS on political and public agendas in the 1980s and 1990s, organisations from developing countries found it difficult to find a common voice and a global expression.

In contrast to the highly effective coalition, much of it driven from developing countries, which came into being around the Cairo and Beijing conferences to achieve a sea change in international and national priorities regarding the status of women in society, an analogous international HIV/AIDS civil society coalition has not emerged with the same strength and profile, in part perhaps because there was not a clear issue around which concrete demands for action could be made.

At the end of the late 1990s, that issue potentially emerged in the form of access to treatment for HIV/AIDS. Arguably for the first time, organisations in the South were able to set out their own agenda, their own demands and their own priorities in response to HIV/AIDS. A combination of chronic lack of access to HIV/AIDS treatments, consistent refusal by Northern drug companies and their governments to allow compulsory licensing of combination therapies, the perceived injustices of international framework of intellectual property rights (TRIPS) and the grow ing scale of the epidemic finally ignited a major international, southern driven political movement to campaign for the rights of people with HIV in developing countries.

The flames of this movement originated principally in South Africa and Brazil in response to the refusal of international pharmaceutical companies to reduce the price of ARVs or allow developing countries to produce them themselves. They were fanned by the political row s surrounding President Thabo Mbeki's unwillingness to acknowledge the reality of the AIDS epidemic in his country, and the lack of commitment to tackling the epidemic by many of Africa's political leaders.

The international HIV/AIDS conference in Durban in 2000, the first such international conference to take place in a developing country and the first where a majority of participants were from developing countries, further energised this movement. Despite the huge practical, as well as economic, constraints of making antiretroviral therapies available in many developing countries, this movement is beginning to provide civil society in developing countries with the opportunity to make the AIDS issue their own, to carve out their own agendas on the epidemic and to transform a health issue into a political one.

In doing so, millions of people in South Africa, Brazil and elsew here who have formerly regarded the issue of HIV/AIDS as one of public health and sexual behaviour have been draw n into a debate marking it out as an issue of economic justice and human rights. International lobbying has led to important concessions by international pharmaceutical companies to reduce the prices of ARVs and most recently to major concessions over intellectual property rights at the World Trade Organization.

AIDS has a history of being a highly political and politicised epidemic, capable of energising social movements in a way that is rarely the case with other health issues. It is clear that lasting impact on HIV/AIDS is dependent on a major global response, but it is equally clear that that response needs to be implemented within the context of a global agenda on the issue which is shaped and driven from within developing countries. The treatment campaign is helping to crystallise that response.

However many activists remain pessimistic over what can be achieved in providing a markedly increased level of access even with significantly increased funding. The UNGASS document stressed both prevention and treatment as key strategies in tackling the AIDS pandemic, and arguments are likely to intensify over coming months over where and how to prioritise resources.

An alternative analysis of the treatment campaign is that the issue, far from politicising the epidemic, is remedicalising it. A major reason for the establishment of UNAIDS was the acknowledgement of the complexity of the epidemic and the clear need for a multisectoral response to it. With the issue of treatment once again moving centre stage, there is a concern that the focus will move tow ards an essentially medical solution, with the focus shifting to treating the symptoms of an epidemic, not its underlying causes.

Access to treatment is far from being the only issue which is galvanising social movements in this way. A grow ing movement to confront HIV/AIDS related stigma is rapidly taking on a new profile and energy, and is emerging from networks of people living with HIV/AIDS, other HIV/AIDS related civil society organisations and is becoming a major priority for international agencies and organisations. UNAIDS has designated the issue as the focus of the next World AIDS Campaign.

Challenge for Communicators

There have been many debates over communication interventions over recent years, and the Communication for Social Change arguments outlined above constitute just one of them. These debates perhaps lead to a more fundamental set of of questions facing communicators. The international community is responding and has responded to the HIV/AIDS crisis and this response provides a possibly unrepeatable opportunity to make major progress in containing HIV/AIDS. A new and welcome atmosphere of urgency and energy has been created by organisations which has helped galvanise the international response. Arguably, there are three responses being proposed by communicators in response to UNGASS and the increased political priority being given to the epidemic.

There is an "emergency" response, with many agencies and highly committed communication practitioners arguing that we have learned a very great deal about HIV/AIDS and human sexual behaviour over the last 15 years and that the epidemic is now so devastating that we need to rapidly scale up the time, resources and energies putting the strategies we've already developed into action on the ground, and less time theorising about what need needs to be done. They argue that the international attention now focused on the epidemic, and funding from donors will not last unless results are achieved rapidly, but the opportunity presents itself now.

While the response to the AIDS fund has been disappointing, nevertheless much larger sums of money from both public and private sources are available and there is a need to dispense these in highly targeted programmes which take the best of what has worked in the past and combine these with innovative new approaches.

The emphasis here is on urgent action and large scale mass mobilisation of resources and programming, a putting into wide scale practice the strategies that have worked in the past. While proponents of this response acknowledge the risks, in terms of potential lack of indigenous ownership of large scale responses of this kind, they argue that the benefits and urgency outw eigh the risk, and in any case African and other governments and societies are increasingly engaged in shaping agendas around the epidemic. On the other hand, there are those who raise fundamental questions about the strategies that have been employed to date and argue that it is precisely the demand for quick, measurable results that has created a field heavily made up of of large, donor driven, top down communication interventions which have, they argue, proved both unsustainable in securing behaviour change and have not addressed the underlying causes of the epidemic.

They argue that the scale and severity of the epidemic, despite the efforts made to contain it, suggests that a reassessment of strategy is necessary. They argue that major international interventions have sometimes been introduced at the expense of communities and societies taking the ownership and leadership of the fights against HIV/AIDS on for themselves. They argue that the issues of sex and sexuality, and the intimate links between HIV and poverty, HIV and discrimination and HIV and marginalisation suggest much more complex, bottom up strategies aimed at community empow erment, horizontal forms of communication and less rigid and sets of interventions. They also argue that the increasing complexity of developing country societies, prompted by greater liberalisation, more complex media systems, and more complex and horizontal communication patterns in society demand fresh thinking and approaches.

Media and Social Change in Arabic World

One of the most fascinating results of the new transnational media is the extent to which they have allowed the reintegration of Arab emigrants into Arab life and society. No longer cut off from their homelands, many Arabs living in the West read Arab newspapers (either in print or on the internet), watch Arab television (MBC, ART, and LBC are available in the United States by satellite and in some areas by cable), and actively seek out Arab sites on the internet. The image is a startling one, but the fact is that there is an online community of

Arabs based simultaneously in London, New York, and many cities of the region.

As the amount of information about the Arab world available outside the Arab world blossoms, location becomes less and less relevant for one to play an active role in modern Arab society. Something as mundane as decreasing prices for international telephone calls play a role as well. For many years, countries have raised the price of or taxed international phone service to subsidize domestic operations. Under World Trade Organization rules, however, international phone tariffs are expected to drop precipitously in the coming years. As they plummet, so too will the costs of faxes and other transmissions of information over phone lines.

Because of relative ease of use and a large installed base, in the intermediate term the telephone may prove more important than the internet as a conduit for new ideas to enter the Arab world and for reports of conditions within the Arab world to reach Arab communities outside. The enlargement of the Arab community to bring Arabs back into contact with their own societies (and doing so increasingly through interactive media, given the growing prevalence of the internet in the United States) has had the remarkable effect of reinserting expatriate Arab intellectuals into the Arab world.

A host of Western-based Arab academics—many of whom left the Middle East to undertake doctoral research and then found employment in the West studying the Arab world—are becoming fixtures in the new Arab media. Western-based Arab newspaper correspondents and columnists also "write back" into the Arab world, and they are clearly affected by their surroundings.

The internationalization of media coverage has, to a great degree, become like a huge exchange program, in some ways making the West more aware of Arab concerns, but in many ways making the Arab world more aware of the political and social mores of the West. There is a remarkable cross-fertilization of ideas taking place between Arab intellectuals in the West and their colleagues remaining in the Arab world, enabled and driven by the new media.

Even within overseas Arab communities, the internet is causing fascinating changes. As anthropologist Jon Anderson points out, online "communities"—chat rooms, bulletin boards, usenet groups, and so forth—are not typical of the societies from which their members have emerged. The online Arab community is disproportionately composed of scientists, engineers, and students; theologians, politicians, and military officials are underrepresented. The result, Anderson reports, is that individuals who at home would yield to the opinions of specialists find themselves venturing into religious and political topics. In so doing they bring the insights and tools of their professional training to the discussion, resulting in a new "creole" discourse that combines elements of discourse from their own places of origin with Western scientific training and scholarly inquiry.

Arabs still in the Arab world can monitor and participate in most if not all of these discussions, although in doing so they are potentially subject to the same sorts of monitoring that characterize all of their internet use. In all of this cross-fertilization, there are two groups involved. The first are bilingual Arabs, resident either in the West or in the Arab world. They have a choice of language in which to communicate, and often they will communicate some kinds of messages in Arabic and others in Western languages, especially English. The second groups, however, consists of a larger group of Arabs who are not bilingual. For this group, the media are considerably more important and more broadening.

The transnational Arab media become not only their link to other Arabs, but also a fundamental link to the rest of the world. Although some dismiss the new ideas as "corrupting," for large portions of the Arab public this link to the rest of the world is both fascinating and desirable.

There remain large segments of the population, however, for which the changes outlined above are irrelevant to their lives. The regional Arab media remain something of a rich man's game, and penetrations beyond the elite level is slight except in wealthy Gulf states. The effects of the "cross-fertilization" of ideas and reintegration of diasporas will be uneven in the short and intermediate term, although the strong desire for transnational media among the elites in country after country suggest that the media will have a strong effect, even if that effect is from the top down.

To date, market forces have played a relatively minor role in Arab countries. State sectors have generally been strong and private sectors have been somewhat weak. States have either owned media outlets outright or orchestrated the existence or demise of these outlets. Advertising revenues—the mother's milk of media production the world over—has been paltry. As former al-Hayat editor Jihad al-Khazen bemoaned, total advertising spending in the Arab world in 1994 was $900 million, while Israel itself had an advertising expenditure of $800 million.

The regional Arabic-language print and satellite-broadcast media described above have seen a marked increase in advertising spending in recent years. In 1997 alone, for example, advertising spending on pan-Arab television grew by 96 percent over the previous year, to $202 million. Between 1995 and 1997, advertising spending in pan-Arab magazines increased by 36 percent, and in newspapers by 14 percent. The total Arab advertising market has enlarged as well, growing from $1.13 billion in 1995 to $1.54 billion in 1997.

The products advertised are familiar to most Americans. The top ten brands advertised in the regional Arab media and in the member states of the Gulf Cooperation Council (GCC) are Toyota, Nissan, Marlboro, BMW, Pampers, Pantene, Hyundai, Ford, and Chevrolet. Pampers is the most-advertised brand on television in this market, followed by Pantene. Toyota leads in newspaper spending, and Marlboro in magazines. By type of product, the most advertised products on pan-Arab television were adult personal hygiene and health products, followed by shampoos and other hair products, and candy and snacks. The foregoing suggests that what is emerging is not merely a Western-style advertising market, but Western-style brand-name development, Western-style consumption patterns, and personal lifestyles that are more Western, at least in their outward manifestations.

This trend toward Westernization is neither a completed process nor a foregone conclusion; in addition, it is hard to foresee how more Western consumption patterns might affect other aspects of Arab life. It has become a trope of Western media reports about Saudi Arabia and Iran to note that veiled women in those countries are sometimes impeccably dressed under their black cloaks, but whether such patterns of dressing (and consumption) reflect a stable situation or one on the verge of change remains unclear.

The shape of Arab media in the future very much depends on the shape of the Arab media market, and that market is dependent on a continued shift toward higher per capita incomes and increasingly Western patterns of consumption. If the media market grows, media outlets will continue to experiment with content to draw more viewers. Arab viewers will likely see more sex and scandal, and political coverage will likely grow more daring, at least in the near and intermediate term (but they will undoubtedly continue to shy away from offending Saudi political sensibilities). Although in the future not all television may resemble LBC or al-Jazeera, the two stations have proved that Arabs thirst for new kinds of programming; meanwhile, the continued high viewership of MBC suggests that even playing things relatively straight can create a powerful media force in the region.

The important thing to keep in mind is that if the media in the Middle East become more market-oriented, they will provide more of what people want to see and read. This will not necessarily be highbrow material, but if the Western experience is any guide, the Arab media will find that pushing boundaries often proves a more successful strategy than staying far away from them. In such a scenario, a more market-oriented Arab media could be expected to be more daring on sex and politics than what has been the case, although one would expect that they would retain some respect for regional mores, at least in the immediate term. If the broadcasts and printed press are too "out there," they merely come across as imports, and that can affect their broad acceptance.

That marketing expenses will rise enough to make broadcasting profitable is by no means certain. Persistently low prices for petroleum products will depress the economies not only of the Gulf states, but also of the countries that export labor to those states. Lack of a marketing infrastructure discourages advertising as well.

In the event that free-to-air stations never become commercially viable, the satellite television market will likely become bifurcated. The first resulting segment would be state-sponsored satellite television. While Qatari-backed al-Jazeera has challenged the status quo, with time and the intervention of governmental interests it seems more likely that the future face of government-sponsored television will be more staid. There will be a strong impetus for states to essentially sign nonaggression pacts regarding their state-run media, and the media will again emerge as the foreign policy tool that they were when Gamal Abdel Nasser first harnessed them in the 1950s and 1960s. Whereas many satellite stations are now based out of Europe, their migration back to the region and increasing government control over their operations will tend to dampen their aggressive news coverage.

The other part of the market likely to survive would comprise the fee-for-service stations like ART and Orbit, driven by high per-user fees and a superior ability to monitor the viewing habits of their wealthy customers. How many such networks the market can sustain and at what level of fees is unclear, but they appear to have identified a way to remain afloat without subsidies from outside parties. For the foreseeable future, these stations seem destined to have their sights fixed mostly on the Saudi market, where incomes are highest and entertainment alternatives the lowest. Whether viewers of such stations will, under the influence of Western-oriented programming, become so unlike their countrymen in dress and speech as to pose a social or political problem for their societies is unclear.

Clearly, factors other than television are influencing Arab behavior; still, the January 1997 arrest of seventy-six young adults in Egypt—many of them students at the American University in Cairo—for "satanic practices" influenced by their watching American music videos on satellite television must be a cautionary tale. In many poorer societies in the Arab world, satellite television is contributing to a phenomenon in which some segments of society are educated and oriented in an entirely different way than the mass of their compatriots.

As an additional result of the increasing market orientation of the Arab media is their likely migration back to the region for at least some of their production. Producing material in high-cost cities like London, New York, and Washington cannot compete economically with the production costs in Amman, Cairo, or possibly Beirut.

Of course, many of the regional Arab media have been shaped by their growth outside the Arab world and are more liberal in their approach to social and political affairs than was common heretofore in Arab countries; extraregional production allows them a somewhat greater degree of freedom of expression. Yet, the time will come, sooner rather than later, when economies will induce these organizations to return to the region. Their move will be eased by the generally more open media environment prevailing in the Arab world. Saudi-run organizations will have the most difficult choice to make, however, because the kingdom is among the least open societies in the region, and the efficiencies of doing business there are among the least compelling.

4

Media and Gender Development

The media is the nerve centre of expression, producing and transmitting information it considers important to society. Through the media, public opinion is generated, strengthened, and nourished. The progress made in recent years by media has opened new possibilities to make women's contribution to society visible. It has enabled women to organize and communicate across national, regional and international boundaries. There has been a fair debate and dialogue in the past years on the nexus between women, media, and communications. There has been criticism on the use of women's bodies to promote sales or increase audience. Several studies have shown that little progress has been made in these issues. But this has not diminished women's work to overcome discrimination, stereotypes, and cultural bias. On the contrary, it has challenged them to work strategically to place their new roles in private and public life, and their contribution to civil society. Women want to build an integral vision of themselves as citizens and subjects of communications with equal rights and opportunities.

Media's Approches to Gender Development

There are different models of communications and ways of influencing the media that women have put into action in many countries around the world in order to make progress in gender equity in the communications arena. They have a multiplier effect; they can be replicated in and adapted to other regions; have a broad participation base; are sustainable and innovative; and represent efforts made by many women and women's organizations to promote change and a positive impact of gender perspective in the media. The best practices discussed in this section have been selected based on the following categories: outreach to media, advocacy, media watch, codes and standards and use of new information and communications technology.

Best Practice Models for Outreach to Media

Women's groups working on media have learnt that building positive relations with media institutions and professionals are essential for improving the portrayal and position of women in media. They know they must move beyond the complaints about the inadequacies of media content, and express constructive criticism.

Many media advocacy groups have realized that one way of getting more women's voices heard in the media is to build strong alliances with sympathetic media professionals – reporters and managers. Forging alliances with media is both a long and short-term goal. The challenge is to ensure that media handles women's concerns, achievements, and activities with a gender perspective and sensitivity, and in a reliable and sustainable manner.

Bringing a gender perspective and sensitivity to media content is a skill. Women's groups have had to and need to be very innovative to keep their concerns in front of the media, while co-operating with media professionals. Most important, there is a great need for continuing education of media professionals, male and female.

The Global Women's Media Team (GMWT) was organized by Isis International-Manila at the UN General Assembly Special Session to review the implementation of the Beijing Platform for Action (UNGASS) in New York from June 5 to 9, 2000. The goal of the project was to cover the issues discussed in the UNGASS, and make it accessible to women's organizations, NGOs and mainstream media. It brought together 13 writer-trainees from women's NGOs, two editor-trainers, a media liaison staff, an administrative staff, and one project co-ordinator. These writer-trainees attended a preparatory workshop and had daily sessions with the editor-trainers as resource people. They wrote news and features, which were disseminated to media, outlets in New York, their own countries and key press agencies. It was unique in that it combined media coverage with actual training. The implementation of the project required effective planning and partnership with different networks and institutions. The GWMT produced 49 stories/press releases in English., some of which were translated into other languages and sent to 168 print, broadcast and electronic media outlets around the world using the Beijing+5-news electronic mailing list and fax. Quite a few of the releases were picked up by several media around the world.

Since UNGASS, team members continued the outreach in their countries. The training component also included a workshop on media monitoring and networking by Gabrielle le Roux of Media Watch South Africa; a hands on workshop on Internet broadcasting by Feminist International Radio Endeavour (FIRE). In retrospect, the project could have benefited from a larger and more timely pool of funds, so that the organizers could do a better job.

Women's Feature Service (WFS) is an international news and features agency covering development issues from a gender perspective. Created in 1978 by UNESCO in conjunction with the UN Decade for Women (1975-85), the goal was to get women's writing and analysis into the mainstream media, and, therefore, to influence policies related to women and development. It was a project of the Inter Press Service; an Italy-based third-world news agency from 1978-90. Since 1991, it has been operating as an independent organization from New Delhi, India. The WFS currently produces 432 news and 480 feature items from 30 countries written by 120 women journalists, the majority of whom are from the South. WFS has systematically covered the UN international and regional women's conferences since 1980 and published a daily newspaper at the Beijing conference and other conferences, providing media coverage in English, Spanish and sometimes French. This has also been offered to regular WFS mainstream media clients. WFS has and continues to conduct on-line training for its writers, and works with various civil society organizations in their outreach to media by offering advice media strategy.

During its Sixteen Days of Activism against Violence against Women, the Kenya based Coalition of Violence Against Women (COVAW-K) first started its work with mainstream media. As a women's human rights organization, it is committed to the eradication of all forms of violence against women and the promotion of women's human rights. Since its formation in 1995, COVAW-K has been working to sensitize women, men, and young people on the issue of violence against women. Through a public debate in the media, the issue of violence against women has been put on the local and national agenda.

The annual global campaign, "Sixteen Days Campaign" has been marked in Kenya for several years now. By deliberately involving the media, it has been possible to promote an open public debate on various aspects of violence against women – to break the silence, to demystify myths, and to challenge repugnant cultural norms. There is an increased awareness among women, men, and youth on the different manifestations of violence against women. Building a rapport with the media was needed so that cases of violence against women would be reported without bias; and to publicize the activities of the Coalition, so that people know where to go to in times of need. The result of this campaign has been tremendous – many women have become aware of the issue and have joined the activities nearest to them. Some people that COVAW assists now came through the media campaign. Journalists are more aware, and COVAW will definitely continue working with the media to keep the debate "alive."

In Bujumbura-Burundi, the Saving Women's Life media campaign was organized around World Population Day 2000. A journalists' network was formed, and government institutions and local NGOs participated. Articles appeared in different newspapers; television and radio shows were produced and aired, and a videocassette about World Population Week 2000 was produced. A debate was broadcast on radio and television; there was a game contest on Reproductive Health; and there were testimonies on cases where organizations saved women's lives (such as the Association of Women Lawyers and the Iteka League). Prizes were given for a drawing contest in schools organized by an UNFPA project for children aged 6 to 18. Posters and banners were put up in Bujumbura on the theme of "Saving women's lives."

In Nepal, the Women's Communicators Group conducted a Gender Orientation Workshop for Media Professionals to encourage gender-insensitive reporting and to discourage the negative portrayal of women. The objective was to establish a common understanding of basic gender concepts among journalists, increase their analytical skills for gender-fair reporting, and to strengthen advocacy for mainstreaming gender in the media. To increase cooperation and build partnerships with journalists' associations, media educators, and gender experts, a training manual was developed in consultation with recognized media educators to ensure ownership of the process. The basic orientation workshop was followed up by a Training of Trainers (TOT) to produce gender trainers out of media professionals. Smaller follow-up workshops were conducted to provide new trainers with opportunities to use what they had learned. A media monitoring exercise followed these sessions. There was a noticeable increase in the coverage of gender issues, and media coverage also became more gender-sensitive.

In Australia, the Media Entertainment and Arts Alliance (MEAA) began research on the status of women working in the media as part of a broader study by the International Federation of Journalists. Its aim was to determine the status of women working in the media and issues affecting their role in media organizations throughout Australia. Three thousand women working in print, radio and television received the survey. It covered recruitment, pay equality, promotion, job segregation, training, and development, working conditions, maternity leave, childcare, sexual harassment, equal employment opportunities and the role and perception of the union.

The MEAA received 368 responses (a response rate of 12.3%). The survey established that the biggest issues are equal opportunity for promotions, childcare, and sexual harassment. There was evidence, for example, that "family responsibilities have an impact upon women's work in the media," with almost 10% saying that they have had to leave a job due to pregnancy-related reasons. Fifty-one percent (51%) said they have had to put up with sexist remarks, gestures, and other forms of harassment that have undermined their confidence and affected their work. With these results in hand, MEAA plans to address the extent of direct and indirect discrimination in the workplace, and to identify contemporary issues that concern women working in the media.

The Tunis-based Centre of Arab Women for Training and Research (CAWTAR) is a reference centre for the Arab region allowing governments and NGOs to integrate a gender approach into their policies and programmes for the advancement of women. It is an information centre working to raise awareness of policy-makers and planners to ensure that more women participate more in decision-making in all fields and levels, and to recognize women's contribution to development.

CAWTAR has launched three contests to select the best article on the themes "Arab women five years after Beijing", "March 8th in the Arab Countries" and "The Greatest Accomplishments for Women in Your Country" and "What is Modernity for Arab Women in the 21st

Century?" The main objective of the first action was to make known the Beijing Platform for Action and contribute to the implementation of the recommendations of the Beijing conference with regard to the fight against discrimination against women, the guarantee of women's rights and the furthering of women's participation in development. Positive reactions to this initiative and the involvement of several partners in making the first contest a success greatly contributed to the success of a second contest, launched in November 2000.

During the first Arab Women's Summit, organized in Cairo, Egypt, last November, the year 2001 was declared "The Year of Arab Women." Using this as a framework, CAWTAR decided to launch its third contest aimed at Arab journalists (written press) to encourage them to follow the events of this year and to reflect on the third theme mentioned above. By organizing these contests, CAWTAR wants to identify journalists who can integrate a gender approach into their writing, and present the diverse images of Arab women's contribution to development. It wants to unite journalists and necessary documentation – treated and furnished by CAWTAR – to produce in-depth articles on priority topics. Through these actions, CAWTAR hopes to help improve the ability of the media for more gender-sensitive reporting and thus to contribute to promote and protect women's rights in Arab countries.

The Arab Women Media Centre in Jordan works mainly to train and educate women in the media so that they can be stronger in the workplace. It also works on media education for non-media personnel and the public. Its aim is to run a media business (prints, audio, video), which focus on women, children and family rights. It houses a media-training centre to help unemployed women in the media to find a job and protect them from being abused by media agencies. The Centre has good links with government and NGO media institutes. Their activities and inputs have been well received by the media and published in daily and weekly newspapers. Local television channels and local and foreign radio stations have also covered the Centre's work.

In Canada, More Than Just a Dozen was a radio project based on the 12 Areas of Concern in the Beijing Platform for Action. Its aim was to develop tools that could be used by trainers and educators for educating secondary school students and others to share the voices of women who have worked and are working internationally in these 12 critical areas. Twenty-four radio programmes (with educational booklets with transcripts for educators), and a CD were produced. These were distributed widely to educators mainly in Canada, but also through development agencies internationally. The booklets are very much in demand, and, along with accompanying radio programs, they have been developed into workshops for teachers. The use of multimedia, the 12 Areas of Concern, as well as its focus on young people, all make this project unique.

Founded in France in 1996, Les Pénélopes are the shock troops of feminist journalism. Their media strategy is based on "invasion": first Internet, then other media. According to Joëlle Palmieri, co-founder of Les Pénélopes, "What Internet has made possible is the creation of our own channel of dissemination. We believe this was a decisive factor. We don't have to depend on a political or economic entity to broadcast. I would go so far as to say that our strategy as women should be to have our own satellite!"

The Pénélopes' Web site, created in 1997, has allowed them to disseminate a large volume of information. Their all-volunteer team searches the planet for news, and what they collect and transmit is largely "unpublished, at least in France, because it is chosen from a gender perspective." This site, and their so-called "media harassment" policy has won them an exceptionally good media coverage: interviews, newspaper articles, and soon requests from media to publish content by Les Pénélopes. Their first deal was for a weekly television program on Canalweb, the first French-language Web-based television station.

Canalweb provided the technical infrastructure and Les Pénélopes provided the content: an hour-long feminist program every week. Making this show for Canalweb gave Les Pénélopes the credibility and the experience they needed to go into production on their own a year later. They started with a bang: during the six days of the Special Session "Women 2000", Les Pénélopes teamed up with WomenAction to offer a genuinely "multimedia" coverage of the event. The Web-TV program welcomed more than 50 women from all regions to discuss topics including media, armed conflict, globalization, health, environment, and Francophonie (the French-speaking world). Since then, they have roamed the planet producing their own open, international, nomadic television program, which they broadcast once a month on their own server.

Although Web-TV is not accessible to the majority of the world's women, their approach has nonetheless been fruitful. Television has a language, a dynamic of its own, one that is familiar to women throughout the world. This dynamic allows women to say things that they would not say in any other media. In addition, the programs that Les Pénélopes produce make up a precious video archive that can one day be disseminated more broadly.

In the meantime, Les Pénélopes are invading other media: a column in the leftist newsweekly Politis gives them a wide dissemination in a written medium, and of course they haven't abandoned the Internet. Since joining European WomenAction in the fall of 1999, they have taken the lead in covering important "official" events (CSW, UNGASS, Davos) as well as "parallel" one such as the World Social Forum in Porto Alegre or the People's Summit of the Americas in Quebec. Their short, snappy articles have crossed the planet, ensuring that women who could not intend were still informed. Palmieri sums up Les Pénélopes' approach to media "We must come on strong, as professionally as possible... our strength is our content and our practices; all we have to do is value them. It is imperative that we have an offensive, even an aggressive, strategy. We have nothing to lose and everything to gain! This is how we can change the image of women in the media: as actors (authors, creators, artists, directors), as subjects (daily life, politics, work, violence...), as audience."

In Mexico, journalists have organized CIMAC (Communication and Information for Women), a multimedia body seeking to influence national and international media, from a gender perspective. Female and male members of CIMAC work to produce and disseminate to the mainstream media information on the status of women, sexual and reproductive health, women's human rights, and violence against women.

CIMAC was founded in 1987, and due to its credibility, was able to create a journalists' network ten years ago. It has a news agency, a documentation centre with an archive of newspapers and publications open to the public. CIMAC also monitors Mexican newspapers; acts as consultant for media outlets and journalists that want to work with a gender perspective; and trains journalists and media practitioners for gender equity.

Best Practice Models for Media Advocacy

In the interactive television studio during the U.N. Special Session "Women2000," New York, June 2000. NGO women from around the world discuss health: on the left, Princesse Happy from Cameroon, on the right, Dominique Foufelle from France.

Advocacy has become an essential part of many women-in-media and communication organizations, and a focus of Section J. Whether it is advocacy to other women's organizations, media, government, other civil society organizations, advocacy is essential to bring about change in how women are portrayed in the media.

In Accra, Ghana, Women's Voices was developed to assess the impact of the implementation of government policy to achieve the Beijing goals. It focused mainly on Ghana's commitment to the areas of health, education, economic empowerment, and female child education. It had aimed to give a voice to women who did not have the opportunity to discuss their concerns and demands.

The programme was developed with community-based women groups, Ghanaian NGOs, and international groups working with women in the communities that were selected for this purpose. Docu-drama was used to play out the economic issues and break down cultural barriers to be able to speak frankly about reproductive health. Interviews, commentaries, personal testimonies, and focus group discussions were part of the dynamics that helped produce radio spots. They are still used to lead discussions on these issues.

In the Philippines, the Philippine Centre for Investigative Journalism (PJIC) created a Women's Desk in 1995 to produce investigative and feature reports on women's issues. Since then, 28 reports have been produced, resulting in credible and reliable documents to which columnists, and public officials have devoted column space and airtime. For instance, in July 1995, the then President Fidel Ramos called for a stop to sex tours after the Desk's exclusive coverage of a secret trip by Australia-based women's advocates to Angeles City, where Australian syndicates were believed to be running a thriving sex tourism business.

In 1996, the Desk produced various investigative reports, dealing with urban poor women struggling to overcome poverty, violence, and AIDS. One of these was selected as a finalist for the first Award for Excellence in Writing on Women and AIDS sponsored by the UN Joint Programme on HIV/AIDS and the AIDS Prevention and Control Project from over 120 international entries, and won second place. The project was a challenge in terms of making editors accept media coverage written from a gender perspective. It was a pleasant surprise to find out that media welcomed their work on issues such as contraception, agriculture, labour, education, health, and nutrition.

In New Delhi, India, the Centre For Advocacy and Research (CFAR) works on advocacy and research in and on the media. It monitors print, radio, television; conducts surveys on emerging trends, and, with the research, creates awareness by media about crucial issues. CFAR's main focus has been television, since the last ten years have seen phenomenal growth in the medium. Before the 1990s, television was State-controlled in India. Currently, there are 40 channels on the air, most held by giant media houses. CFAR monitors news and current affairs, soaps and serials, situation comedies and talk/chat/game shows, all of which require separate standards, and an understanding of how each genre works in the Indian context. Monitoring tools are revised to keep pace with developments in programming styles and content. Its monitoring is supplemented with audience research to ascertain what viewers watch, how they watch, when they watch, and how a programme affects them. Interaction with audience groups has resulted in publishing documentation on viewer preference, and in providing these groups with an identity and with high awareness of their rights as consumers.

The monitoring and research information is used for advocacy. CFAR set up Viewers Forums in the North Indian cities of New Delhi, Lucknow, Ahmedabad and Mau for viewers to state their opinions in an organized, timely manner. It has created advocacy training modules for grassroots practitioners, with simple and effective how-to's for interacting with media, presenting issues lucidly and comprehensively, and retaining media interest in the process. Four training modules were prepared on Television Images and Policy, Advertising, Media Laws and Technology.

The Forum dialogues regularly with policy makers, channel managers, directors, producers, actors, advertisers and regulatory bodies within the industry. The members of the Forum produce a regular newsletter called Viewers' Voices in English and Nazariya (meaning Viewpoint) in Hindi. CFAR has access to government policy makers, heads of broadcasting among the state and private networks, and programme managers, keeping them informed of programme trends, audience opinion, and related happenings. It keeps these crucial channels of communication open, so broadcasters who are establishing new norms and practices become more inclusive and gender-sensitive.

In Cairo, Egypt, the Population Council and Future's Group International organized a communications activity with the aim of increasing reproductive health information in Arab newspapers and publications. The objective was to create a network of journalists specialized in this issue, enhancing their knowledge of specific areas related to population and reproductive health issues; improving the content and the quality of reporting in the Egyptian Arabic language press; and increasing the coverage of reproductive health issues in selected daily and weekly leading newspapers and magazines in Egypt. It also aimed to strengthen the professional network of talented journalists interested in and committed to covering reproductive health issues.

The activities implemented consisted of four round tables with key researchers as speakers; the compilation of a packet of resource materials distributed to the journalists who attended the round tables; and brainstorming to start thinking about the type of articles that could be written on the issues. Regular contacts and follow-up with journalists occurred after each meeting.

Every day, press clippings were taken from all the newspapers and magazines that the group members represented, as well as others, and were reviewed regularly. A content analysis of the press clippings was conducted to examine the number of articles and quality of coverage. This was useful in determining the overall space devoted to these issues in the Egyptian press, and the depth and variety of information presented. The network of journalists created through this project is still active and allows the regular exchange of information on reproductive health issues. Due to the success of this communications activity, it was decided to replicate the project in Jakarta, Indonesia, and in Dhaka, Bangladesh.

In Haiti, the Women's Desk of the Centre for Research and Action for Development (CRAD) and its Information Service (SICRAD) publish a monthly popular magazine on gender issues called KOME: journal popile fanm. The Women's Desk works mainly with rural women on education and health issues from a gender perspective, and is involved in the struggle of Haitian women for democracy and the right to freedom of expression. Kome is a space for women to discuss issues and cover activities of women's organizations. The magazine has good links with community based organizations and radio stations. It is published in Creole, Haiti's national language. It also has an audio and electronic component. The audio version reaches mainly rural women, mostly illiterate. Women are encouraged to contribute information, opinion columns, and articles.

A series of successful National Communications Campaigns have been organized by Calandria, a communications NGO from Lima, Peru. The campaigns started in 1996 and have focused on women's rights and struggles against discrimination. Calandria's team realized that it was necessary to enhance their education, awareness, and lobbying tasks with a campaign that could reach media, and use communications tools to get to the people.

The campaigns included a survey in which several issues were probed: gender equity in Congress; perceived progress in the Beijing+5 process; women and political participation in municipal elections, etc. The results of these surveys were presented as part of a public event. Video, booklets, and leaflets are used to present the issues to grassroots people in the city, suburbs and rural areas. The survey results are sent to the main newspapers, and radio and TV spots are produced for national broadcast. Video debates take place in inland towns and villages and in the main squares in big cities.

The campaigns have created a favourable climate for education on citizenship and civil rights; promoted women's participation at the municipal levels; and created a better environment for women politicians. In Cuenca, Ecuador, three organizations hold an annual contest: Women: Image, and Testimonies. Since 1994, ALDES, HABITierra and SENDAS have come together every year to make visible and re-evaluate the participation of women in society regarding gender equity. The contest was national until 1999, but, since the year 2000, has become regional with the participation of writers and photographers from the Andean countries.

The contest consists of testimonies on women's lives and experiences, as well as photographs on women. Women and men can take part in the contest. They belong to popular organizations, trade unions, student unions, housewives' leagues, professional associations, etc. Over 448 writings and 194 photos were presented last year. All writings that are selected and awarded become part of a publication and go from town to town, encouraging debate, meetings, and communication events. Radio scripts are based on the testimonies and programmes for broadcast. The organizers feel that this contest has contributed to gender equity, helping value the role of women in family and society. It has enhanced women and men's perception of gender relations, and the will to overcome discrimination, stereotypes, and bias. Women have been empowered, and see themselves as social actors with equal rights and opportunities.

Best Practice Models for Media Watch

Monitoring the media is a new and important tool for citizens' participation. Globalization and concentration of media have made it difficult for diverse and minority views to be reflected in such media. Thus, media monitoring is not only important for content analysis, but also for creating awareness that citizens have the power to interact with media, to have opinions on media products, and to have the right to question media messages and propose alternatives.

Women's groups have proved that monitoring provides inescapable evidence of continued imbalances in media representation of women and men in terms of status and authority. By using this evidence in a positive way, women can open up dialogue with the media so as to promote positive changes. Monitors are mirrors held up to the media. They expose warts and flaws, but can similarly show areas for improvement and where they exist, as well as successes that are worth lauding and emulating. Media monitors/watches are not just an essential part of furthering women's rights but of ensuring the full flowering of democracy. Journalism is a public service and monitors ensure that the public is served well with a plurality of views and opinions that will empower them to make informed choices and decisions.

In the years 1995 and 2000, one day was selected for a world-wide media monitoring. It was co-ordinated by the Global Media Monitoring Project of the World Association for Christian Communication (WACC). In 1995, MediaWatch Canada also took part in the co-ordination of this project. On January 18, 1995, this monitoring took place in 71 countries. On February 1, 2000, 70 countries participated. The main results did not vary: in 1995, women represented 17% of the news subjects on radio, television and newspapers on that day, whereas, in 2000, they were 18% against 83 and 82% of men respectively.

Hundreds of volunteers in all the participating countries carried out the monitoring, following specific guidelines. The broad aims of the project, apart from obtaining concrete results, were to strengthen solidarity, media literacy, and advocacy on media and gender issues. According to the organizers, the first global monitoring project helped to demystify research, providing women's networks, media activists, students, and development communication groups with the opportunity and tools to monitor gender representation in the media. The second project took it a step further and researched new issues and extended the usefulness of the research by giving the monitoring groups a more contextual analysis, including country results, for their own education and advocacy work.

Conclusions regarding these monitoring experiences show the need to use the results and go beyond them, to develop interpretations and insights that can help media professionals and media audiences recognize the subtle ways in which gender representation is constructed. These would help have a constructive dialogue with media professionals, media literacy initiatives, and continued monitoring to keep track of progress. The conclusions have been published and can be also found on the Internet.

Women's Media Watch started its work in Cape Town, South Africa in 1995. Its activities include media monitoring, advocacy, activism, media and gender awareness workshops, as well as the production of newsletters, documentaries, and radio programmes on equal opportunities for women in the media.

Women's Media Watch believes that the media has the potential to play a meaningful role in this process of nation-building by shifting their paradigm around who and what is newsworthy, and reporting and entertaining in ways that recognize the diversity of the people of their country. Its members act as a media watchdog. Their activism and voice consistently put pressure on the media to commit to change.

In China, in March 1996, a group of women journalists affiliated with the Capital Women Journalists' Association (CWJA) began a Media Monitoring Project. The group conducted several surveys about the news coverage of women in the mainstream media, published essays and research on women's alternative and mainstream media, and started a telephone hotline in 1997 to encourage public participation in media watching. It also joined debates on television and radio programmes, and in newspapers like the China Women's News, a national daily. It has conducted gender-training workshops with minority women journalists, government officials, and the general public.

CWJA has organized seminars on gender sensitivity and media reporting for national and foreign press representatives and government officials. Leaders of the All China Women's Federation also held a round-table discussion with editors-in-chief of major national news media and raised the problems of gender insensitivity and discrimination in the coverage of women's issues. Although some of those who attended were not as receptive, there were others who echoed the results of the meeting with their respective department heads.

Some important results of the monitoring activities included the establishment of a sub-society of women journalists from ethnic minorities, and, on March 8, 2000, CWJA called on all major media in Beijing to allow women to become editors for the day. Several newspapers heeded the call.

The Gender Studies Centre, an information centre and library in Prague, Czech Republic, started the first women's Web site in Czech and Slovak languages, Femininismus.cz, in 1998. It plans to publish information on the status of women in the country and to inform the public and the media about women's activities and issues. This Centre uses the Web site as an alternative medium, publishing news, and information, which would be censored in the mainstream media. It monitors media production and publishes a column called "Chauvinist Bomb of the Week" where papers, TV and radio shows and commercials portraying women in a negative and stereotypical manner are listed and commented on.

The MediaCritic Network "Everything is Possible" was started in Gothenburg, Sweden in 1992 as a reaction to the diminishing and stereotypical portrait of women in Swedish media. With 70 members, its aim is to create awareness in media consumers, so they act responsibly by reacting to gender portrayals with which they disagree. The group has various strategies: forming an enlightened group to learn how to analyze the media; reporting discriminatory materials to the Swedish Council against Gender Discrimination; sending reaction postcards to media producers, and lecturing far and wide about gender portrayal to media practitioners, teachers, gender equality workers, etc.

In Canada, the National Watch on Images of Women in the Media (MediaWatch) Inc is a bilingual (French and English) media-monitoring organization. It became an autonomous organization in 1983, originating as a sub-committee of the National Action Committee on the Status of Women. National Committee members are women who are experts in their fields. MediaWatch relies on their expertise and contacts to ensure that it can successfully reach its goals. Its main objective is to have a media environment in which women are realistically portrayed and fairly represented in all their physical, economic, racial and cultural diversity. It does this by educating media industries, government, and the public. It conducts research and encourages community action.

In a recent research project in partnership with the University of Toronto it investigated the response of "tweens" (11 - 14 year old girls) regarding the effect of media on body image and self-esteem. The results were distributed to appropriate groups/individuals/agencies to be used to educate the general public, media organizations, and industry regulators. Over the years, MediaWatch has influenced public policy, educated and mobilized consumers to advocate for change and contributed substantive research to the field. Through research analysis and public education, MediaWatch works with and trains health professionals, educators, researchers, students, community members, and media and industry personnel on how certain media portrayals of women and girls affect individuals' body image and self-esteem of individuals.

In South America, four women's organizations from Chile, Argentina, Paraguay and Uruguay came together to work in a media-monitoring project that would include press, radio and TV in each of their countries. After producing common guidelines and questionnaires, in June 1999 they put their monitoring project into action. Their findings have not differed from results of other monitoring experiences.

But, for the women's organizations, it was very interesting to compare the results between countries and to plan together future lobby actions. They consider their contribution to be to generate independent information that is not dominated by market interests. Since most studies about media are related to commercial interests, they found it necessary to produce alternative information about the media that responds to social interests. They also considered it important to have quantitative data on women's presence in the media, to analyze under what circumstance women appear in the media, and how they are represented.

Women's Media Watch, Jamaica (WMW) was founded in 1987 as a non-government, non-partisan, voluntary organization, to increase public awareness of the causes of sexual violence against women and girls, of violence in general, and to draw links between violence in media images and sexual violence.

The general work of the organization includes an outreach programme based on popular education comprising discussions, workshops and seminars in schools, third-party institutions, with community groups, and with media practitioners locally and regionally; media monitoring and research studies on the representation of gender in mainstream media; lobbying and dialogue with members of the advertising and media communities; the production of resource materials (print and audio-visual) on gender issues and the media and participation in national, regional, international conferences and for a on gender and media.

Over the past twelve years WMW has conducted over 400 workshops and training sessions, locally and regionally, where some 10,000 persons have participated in these face-to-face exercises. An undetermined number of persons have been reached via the local mainstream media. Through such activities, WMW's focus has been deliberately on developing media critiquing skills, gender-sensitivity, and media awareness in its target audience. Over the years WMW has received calls from citizens, asking for its help in lobbying against negative and stereotypical images of women in media programmes. The majority of these persons have participated in one or more of WMW's outreach programmes.

Best Practice Models for Media Codes and Standards

Will media accept and adopt a code of conduct and ethics that specifically addresses gender-fair reporting? What exist are general codes and guidelines that deal with morality, good taste, and decency – concepts which, as women activists and media professionals point out, are open to subjective interpretation.

In recent years, however, there have been initiatives by women's groups and media professionals to address the lack of guidelines regarding coverage of women and women's issues. While these efforts have not yet produced codes duly signed and adhered to by media entities, they have nonetheless paved the way for open and frank discussions on the issue of gender-sensitive media coverage, particularly on issues such as violence against women. There is growing recognition that such codes will not only help upgrade women's status, but also help raise the quality of journalism in general. It should be stressed that the media need to learn that mainstreaming is a process and that gender can be a key tool or activity strategy to effect organizational change, especially in the voices and perspectives provided in its editorial coverage.

Since its creation in 1964, the Inter Press Service (IPS) has become a major information provider, promoting human rights, democracy, and good governance through its innovative system of inter-cultural communication. Its project "Strengthening Gender Perspectives in IPS News Coverage" provided the agency with the opportunity to incorporate gender in a more systematic and planned approach starting in 1995. IPS started a process of examining gender roles and responsibilities within the organization, and the creation of a gender-responsive editorial and employment policy to guide the agency's work toward better practices. At the same time, the training (seminars and on-line training by the editors) of the its journalists on gender and development issues and concepts. In 1995 and 1996, mechanisms were implemented to increase the number of women participating in IPS activities at all levels. In 1996, the agency began developing a gender policy, and in 1997 it developed strategies and training to ensure implementation of the policy.

It focused its attention on improving the gender perspective and women's voices in coverage by IPS journalists of all issues. Training programmes were designed specifically. General guidelines on portrayal, sources and use of data were developed, and a gender glossary was produced in English and Spanish. A set of gender guidelines for journalists was produced and regional gender teams were then set up to continue dialogue on policy and to assist with policy implementation The IPS experience in mainstreaming gender has meant new partnerships with organizations working in women's rights as human rights, gender, and development. These organizations have become key sources of information to IPS journalists and also have been partners in the development of seminars and training programmes for the correspondents and editors.

Isis International was established in 1974 with the goal of providing women with alternative channels of communication. Five years after the formulation of the Beijing Platform for Action, Isis International-Manila organized national and regional workshops on women and the media to review developments in the field since the Platform for Action. It found that there were some media codes with provisions on gender. However, most of these either contained general provisions that pertained to taste, decency, and morality or reinforce the traditional roles assigned to women. None identified stereotyping of women as a problem, or stressed the need to project more diverse and empowering images of women. The workshop participants emphasized the need to produce minimum regional standards in relation to women and the media.

At a 2001 workshop in Malaysia to discuss this subject, two key objectives were identified. The first one was to examine and share experiences on how gender-fair provisions can be incorporated into media codes and enforced. The second was to develop strategies for establishing, incorporating and implementing minimum standards for media codes of conduct at the regional level, given the cultural differences and diversity within the region. It was also discussed whether gender fair codes of conduct would run contrary to freedom of expression; and whether media codes should be self-regulatory or State-imposed.

A key result of the dialogue was the identification of gender principles for media at the regional level to be adapted at the national level. The participants agreed that governments' attempts to impose their own version of morality through a state-sponsored code could even reinforce gender stereotypes. Internal or self-regulatory mechanisms, they said, would be more effective.

The Australian Women in Television Project started in 1997, with project activities in the capital city-states of New South Wales, Victoria, South Australia, and Queensland. The Australian Film Commission (AFC) conducted research in 1996, in which 52 senior women in Australian television were interviewed by telephone to know about what had helped their career advancement, what barriers had they overcome, and any strategies that they thought would assist other women in television to advance their careers. Focus group discussions with women at mid-career level in television were also held in Melbourne and Sydney to obtain feedback on the information obtained from the telephone interviews. Almost all of the women interviewed (90%) said that women were underrepresented in senior positions across Australian television, saying that informal networks would assist in reversing this situation. Other suggested skills development programmes, the establishment of a mentoring programme, and promotion of strategies for how to balance work and family while in the industry. The research outcomes were discussed with the major

Australian television networks and they all agreed to work co-operatively with the AFC.

As a result of this project, approximately 200 women annually have been provided with the opportunity to network with others working in similar areas in television. The project has diversified from networking functions to skills development workshops, the publication of a book *Shared Visions: Women in Television*, and a soon-to-be published booklet of case studies on strategies for balancing work and family while working in television. A mentoring programme for women working in television has been funded by the Australian Film Commission, and will be undertaken by Women in Film and Television (WIFT), a national NGO.

The Al-Quds Educational TV, of the Institute of Modern Media of Al-Quds University, in Ramallah, West Bank, Palestine, developed two projects to promote a balanced and non-stereotypical image of women in Palestinian and Arab media. The first was a series of six 15-minute documentaries related to Gender and Development. Six characters (men, women, educated and non-educated, and non-popular) were chosen to be role models. Each film shows a profile of these women and men practising their normal life. Topics discussed were promoting gender concepts in the Palestinian local community, women's right for education, loans and micro-enterprises for the support of women, oral political history and the role of Palestinian women throughout 1930-1950 and stories of women political activists. The documentaries were shown on TV and are also used in workshops in different locations, especially camps and villages. Women's organizations use them as tools to promote women's participation in social and political life and their recognition as key actors in the life of their country.

The second was training workshops with Palestinian journalists on issues such as gender and human rights, gender and media, gender and TV production, in the framework of the Convention for the Elimination of All Kinds of Discrimination Against Women (CEDAW). Workshops resulted in the production of a TV talk show entitled "Palestinian women and Media coverage." It included four field reports on Palestinian women portrayal in advertising, TV series, local TV programmes, and the role of Palestinian women journalists in news coverage. It was distributed to seven TV stations in the West Bank and Gaza, including the government owned TV (Land Channel and Satellite Channel).

Best Practice Models for ICTs

The information revolution has given birth to the World Wide Web, satellite and cable TV, desktop publishing and electronic networking via the Internet. It has paved the way for press freedom and democracy in many countries in the world. ICTs have also enabled women's groups with diverse interests and agendas both within countries and across borders to come together. They have discovered the liberating power of the Internet and its rich possibilities. Many women's NGOs who went online say they have benefited by gaining more visibility through Web sites, having access to donor assistance, and information especially of international and regional activities, relating to the women's movement. Reports point to the fact that ICTs have given women employment. Yet, despite these reported gains, there are more women on the other side of the digital divide, without access to ICTs. Structural barriers such as poverty, uneven economic development, language, and technophobia further exacerbate the situation.

There is also a growing concern that the information revolution is creating a new world communications order that is being shaped and dominated by big transnational corporations that care more about profit than public service. Fears have been expressed that the commercialization of media could lead to the marginalization, even death, of small, indigenous media outfits that cater to voiceless sectors, including women.To address ICT gaps and inequalities, a number of NGOs around the world have made it their special mission to help women understand ICT and equip them with the necessary tools that they can use to help themselves.

The processes of the UN Decade for Women (1975-85), the Fourth World Conference on Women (1995), and the UN Special Session in June 2000 also started a trend. It helped direct women's groups to make use of new ICTs in ordeuse of new ICTs in order to share news, activities, and information; to network for lobbying and advocacy, and to organize their participation during major UN meetings where issues of interest for women were discussed. The Women's International Network (WIN) of the World Association of Community Radio (AMARC) used e-mail effectively for strategic and preparatory discussions for their participation at Beijing+5. The AMARC office in Montreal initiated, animated and summarized the discussion in which about ten women participated actively for four months, in English, French and Spanish. During this, they were able to, among other things, prepare a position paper on AMARC-WIN for Beijing +5 on Section J; write an alternative world report on Chapter J on Community radio; co-ordinate the participation of the different members of AMARC-WIN at the Beijing+5, and decide on activities in New York. From this experience, WIN members realized the potential of their network for active participation in a major discussion with an active facilitator to moderate it. They effectively repeated the experience again in November 2000 to submit a project proposal to UNIFEM for a Radio Campaign against violence against women.

The Women's International News Gathering Service (WINGS) is based in Austin, Texas, USA, and involves radio stations in the US, Canada, Australia, New Zealand, Ireland, South Africa, and Costa Rica, and short-wave and Internet distribution reaching most of the world where technology to receive it is available. WINGS was founded in 1985 to continue coverage of the global women's movement, after the UN Decade End Conference for Women. It arose out of the context of the women's news movement that began on local community radio in the early 1980s, the creation of AMARC and the US National Federation of Community Broadcasters. The objectives were to create and maintain regular time slots for women's information, voices, issues, and actions, on non-commercial radio across the English-speaking world. It also aimed to increase understanding within the women's movement of the importance of using media and to train, help and raise awareness among women reporters and producers from the grassroots to the professional level. WINGS is eager to help other women get involved in radio production and access radio technologies.

WomenAction 2000 grew out of a Global Communications Forum held during the first Preparatory Commit Preparatory Commission meeting for the Beijing Platform for Action Review (Beijing+5) in March 1999. The discussions focused on how the organizations and networks could keep in touch during this process and collaborate in order to widen women's participation.

All activities for the UNCSW in March 2000, and the UNGASS, in June 2000, were discussed and co-ordinated by e-mail. The group at these forums included women journalists, editors, translators, technicians, Webmasters, designers, radio and TV producers, trainers, and women skilled in Internet tools to distribute news and information widely. The main efforts of the WomenAction team were directed towards producing the daily newspaper for print and electronic distribution, running the Internet café for NGO delegates, and co-ordinating the Women and Media Caucus's efforts to effect substantive revisions in the Outcomes Document of the UNGASS.

The Feminist International Radio Endeavour (FIRE) and Les Pénélopes, a French feminist organization that produces interactive TV programmes ran their own media and communication activities in cooperation with WomenAction, making this project a multimedia effort. Thousands of women in New York and other regions received daily informatly information.

Women'sNet, based in South Africa, aims to make technology accessible to women, particularly those who have been historically disadvantaged. It provides responsive, gender-sensitive training and support, create strategic links between projects and organizations working around women's issues, provide a platform for women's voices and facilitating the dissemination of information in formats that are accessible to women who are not directly linked to the Internet. The rationale behind developing the community radio project was to improve the flow of gender content in programming and news.

Women's Net organized a series of workshops to develop the capacity of women's/gender organizations to handle the media. Participants learned how to use field recorders, how to improve their interviewing skills, and how to put together an "interactive" (in the non-technical sense) programme. They learned about digital formatting and editing. Participants were encouraged to think about gender issues, and adjust their programming accordingly. This workshop gave Women'sNet further opportunity to learn about the divergence of cultural influences and how influences and how these impact on radio workers' programming. It got an insider's perspective and understood community radio better. Although the nature of the workshop resulted in very difficult and "sticky" moments, both parties (organizers and participants) left with a good understanding, and new perspectives.

The Women Connect! Project took place in Zimbabwe, Zambia and Uganda, bringing about greater empowerment of women through the effective use of communication. It developed a small grant programme, which benefited 26 projects in three countries. Among these were the Women and AIDS Support Network, Zimbabwe; The Zambia National Association of Disabled Women: and Isis-WICCE, Uganda. Other projects included a grassroots newsletter addressing community needs in reproductive health knowledge and services; a community publishing involving villages in producing media on AIDS, domestic violence and rape; and a media campaign on women's rights launched during an annual advocacy event called "16 Days of Activism."

Famafrique is the Web site of French-speaking African women created in July 1999 as an initiative of the NGO, Enda-Synfev. It contains a variety of information in

Freninformation in French on women and ICTs. In this way, women's organizations of the region are given a space in which their activities and organizations can have greater visibility, and help to master ICTs. A set of documents has been put on line for this purpose.

Famafrique receives 4,000 to 8,000 visits per week. The electronic newsletter, 'La toile d'elles' provides its roughly 390 subscribers with a multitude of information on different fields of interest to them, national and international meetings, important news regarding women in French-speaking Africa and elsewhere. Enda-Synfev has organized workshops on networking and ICTs in French-speaking Africa. The other activities in this programme are a partnership with various organizations with regard to the Beijing follow-up, the best known of which are: Flamme "network of African women online involved in the Beijing + 5 process in Africa" and WomenAction a global network of electronic "women and media [networks] involved in the Beijing+5 process".

In the telecentres that are popping up all over Africa, women need to be able to obtain information; yet they are not using the facilities, because:

a) most of them cannot read;

b) tt read;

b) there is nothing available in their own language;

c) there is nothing available on the subjects in which they are interested; and

d) no one believes that they can handle computers.

The International Women's Tribune Centre is working with women and community groups in Uganda on a project that hopes to reach rural women who are "out of the loop".

As is the case in many countries, Ugandan rural women had to leave school extremely young and therefore have limited reading skills. When they are not in the fields growing food, they are selling food stuff by the road or in the market, caring for the children, cleaning, cooking, etc. But they have made it clear that they want to know about the world and about subjects that concern them in their daily lives.

The challenge was to develop something that would not require reading ability, that "spoke" to them in their own language, and that did not require extensive computer skills. All that the women need to learn to be able to use the programme is how to move and click the mouse. They click graphics – either faces or services or products – and then listen to a voice speaking to them in their local language.

The field-testing that has already taken place has shown that the women wn that the women can handle a mouse. They were delighted to have access to information in their own language, via the spoken word, especially as everything was spoken by local women. It meant they could at last use the computer despite not speaking or understanding English, nor being able to read very well even in their own language. This project therefore uses a CD-ROM format and browser software that can be loaded directly onto the servers in each telecentre. The user has the advantages of Web-page movement and shortcuts to various sections, without the disadvantages of possible slow downloading times, etc.

The subject of the first package of materials is small business, the subject most requested by rural women in several parts of Uganda. Called "Rural Women in Africa: Ideas for Earning Money", it is not a training manual, but rather a collection of ideas to spark discussion and encourage other ideas. IWTC hopes that it will be the first of many such "computer books", available at any time for individual women or groups of women at the telecentres (and internet cafes, women's community groups, etc.) in many parts of Africa where computers are becoming increasingly available to local women, using local languages and appropriate gs and appropriate graphics as needed. Other issue areas women wanted to know about included Women's Human Rights, Women and Peace Activities, and Women and HIV/AIDS.

The Asian Women's Resource Exchange (AWORC) is the result of a workshop organized by Isis International-Manila in 1998. It is an Internet-based women's information service and network in Asia, geared towards developing co-operative approaches and partnerships in increasing access and exploring applications of new information and communication technologies (ICTs) for women's empowerment. It is focused on lobbying and awareness raising campaigns on poverty alleviation, promotion of women's human rights and overall women's empowerment as outlined in the Beijing Platform for Action (BPFA). It provides avenues for women to develop skills in using new ICTs to enhance their areas of work and to use Internet facilities for greater access to information, analyses, and resources to various sectors of women for solidarity building, strengthening gender analyses, analyses, and developing partnerships.

The Korean Women Electronic Network Training (KWENT) was organized by the Asian and Pacific Women's Information Network Center (APWINC), in Sookmyung University, to promote women-related communication technologies for gender equality and equity. APWINC provides a Web-based information service to exchange ICT and women-related information. It promotes ICT education and training at three levels: dissemination, specialization, and globalization.

The Centre de documentation sur l'éducation des adultes et la condition féminine (CDEACF) from Quebec, Canada, launched in 1998, au féminin, a long-term Internet project. Its goal was to help women use information and communications technologies as instruments of their own empowerment. CDEACF held meetings and consultations and published articles and flyers to help women understand how the Internet could help them in their work Around 500 women have been trained in the past two-and-a-half years. CDEACF has been able to obtain equipment and connectivity for over 100 women's groups. It has installed a self-sustaining, high-speed Interneg, high-speed Internet connection for a dozen women's federations in the Maison Parent-Roback.

It has provided the creation of a global network for francophone women activists, feminist scholars and students. It includes an interactive, resource-intensive Web site as well as several specialized discussion lists (netfemmés for women in general, netjeunes for young women, techno on women and technology, dialogues on bridging the language barrier, francofem on international issues involving French-speaking women). It offers consulting services and phone support to groups on new technology issues. It intends to create a critical mass of women's groups that are equipped, connected and well-versed in new technologies. In the community served by Netfemmes, the project has had an important multiplier effect: the Web training has led several groups either to create or to maintain Web sites.

CDEACF has helped groups create and learn to moderate mailing lists, either on its servers or using free services such as egroups. These are all-volunteer groups like the Youth Committee for the Fédération des Femmes du Québec and for coalitions like the World March, which use several lists on the server to co-ordinate r to co-ordinate activities provincially and internationally, and for a group of women in non-traditional professions (Femmes regroupées en options non traditionnelles) who now uses the Internet to build a virtual community for these isolated professional women.

In Northern Ireland, WomensLink is an Internet e-mail list developed in July 1997 by women from community-based women's groups. WomensLink's objectives are to link up women's organizations and activists in Northern Ireland and the border counties of the Republic of Ireland to share and exchange information and to work together on issues of common concern. More than 40 subscribers currently use the Internet mailing list to share news and information. Use of WomensLink has resulted in many collaborations and partnerships within the women's community sector in Northern Ireland. For example, cross-border, cross-community exchanges where a Mother and Toddler Group in Belfast was able to make contact and visit a similar group in Donegal (Republic of Ireland). WomensLink subscribers recently voted online to extend the list to the rest of Ireland, making it an all-Ireland list.

In California, USA, the Salvation Army and Soroptimis Army and Soroptimist International started a programme to train women and youth from the Hispanic community in computer technologies. The programme is called "Get Access – a Women & Youth Computer Skills

Training Program for under-served Hispanics." It aims at providing technology training to those who do not have access to the basic skills by furnishing the means to the community where it is needed most. "Get Access" uses the resources of the computer technology industry to model a program of self-confidence, career paths and offering the tools and technology.

In Winnipeg, Canada, The Women's Television Network (WTN) created WTN Foundation Inc. to ensure that girls and women were provided with the opportunities necessary to take their full place within the Canadian broadcasting system. The programs provided by the WTN Foundation cross several generations and offer a life-long learning approach. It fully funds the Girls TV Camps and Clubs. It is free and for those girls from low-income families, girls whose families have recently immigrated to Canada, girls who are struggling at school, girls from culturally diverse communities. There is a program for girls who graduate from both the camp and tcamp and the club for staff jobs as junior camp counsellors. The Travelling Girls Documentary Team is for graduates of the camp/club. They attend conferences and events across Canada, which promote women and technology. At these events the girls' videotapes the conference events and edit on computers to create a documentary shown at the end of the conference. The girls also participate as speakers on panels.

The Women's TechNical Internship is for women just launching careers in broadcasting and for broadcast employers looking to create a diverse workforce. Partner schools who support the values of diversity in the workplace promote WTNI in their schools and encourage women to apply. Together WTN and the partner schools choose a candidate. The WTN Foundation then pays for half the apprentice's salary in a technical position for six months at the workplace of her choosing (excluding WTN). To date 45 women have launched careers under this program. In any given year anywhere between 75 and 100% of them continue with the employer after the internship period ends or use their new-found skills to land an even better job in the industry. The wtndowment is for older women trying to catch up to the technical evolution and need financial need financial support for re-training. Women from across Canada who've been working in the broadcast industry for at least five years are invited to submit their homespun, personal education plan.

The Asociación de Comunicaciones Feminist Interactive Radio Endeavor (AC FIRE) began broadcasting on short-wave in 1991 with high-quality, non-sexist, activist programs in Spanish and English for radio and the Internet. In 1998, it began its innovative Internet Radio initiative. Today, people around the world can hear about AC FIRE on local radio programmes and stations, in magazines, on the Internet and in workshops and classrooms internationally.

FIRE's goal is to amplify the voices and ideas of women by participating in networks, and in local, regional and global initiatives. Its Web page is a media venue where one can hear, see and read women's voices about all issues. Monthly in-depth features give women's perspectives about issues, identities, cultures, and countries. All reports since 1998 are archived. The combination of text images and embedded sound files for "on-demand" listening, all form a unity where the voices of the women are central. Texts that can Texts that can easily be read on the air on any other radio (compliment) and contextualize what women themselves say about a specific issue.

The Internet features are turned into written articles published every year in its magazine Women's Voices on FIRE. They are also available on the FIRE Web page; others are new or updates of the original Web features.'FIRE organizes special Webcasts from conferences and events. One example is the FIRE-PLACE at the Beijing+5 UN process. Co-ordinated with WomenAction, "Voices without Brackets" was webcast from the building across the United Nations in New York every day between June 4—9, 2000. Women guest producers from around the world hosted programs, focusing on the role of media in relation to the 12 critical areas of concern of the Beijing Platform for Action. In 2000, FIRE began to develop another kind of Webcast - marathons between 12 to 25 hours of uninterrupted programming on special days such as International Day Against Violence, International Women's Day, International Women's Health Day, etc.

Women around the world are invited to send their material about the issue that FIRE will broadcast on that day. Radio stations and other Webcasting Webcasting initiatives are invited to link live in a simultaneous way. The Internet audience is also invited to both listen in and write to FIRE and to the women they hear on FIRE, and especially to multiply the information gathered.

Media's Stand onViolence against Women

Violence and trafficking of women for flesh trade or forced labour in the 21st century continues to blot the human civilization but has not prevented the people from committing crimes against women. This has remained a problem for ages and the continuation of the same is an evidence that concerted efforts have been far too short in rooting out the disdainful practice of treating women as second rate sex object.

In the context of the media, the following are the main reasons for the downplay of women's issues in the mainstream media. Although the convergence of new media technologies and influx of private media organisations in the last decade has increased the number of women working in both print and electronic media, women have not yet gained parity with men in terms of participation and decision-making. Top management is still entirely male-dominated and patriarchal with only a negligible number of women holding senior positions. Although women have become more visible particularly in radio and television as presenters, announcers and reporters, the gender division of labour is highly pronounced in production, creative and technical departments, which are male dominated.

The presence of women is also absent in any official commissions, boards or committees formed for formulating policies or monitoring the media. Recently, as a result of strong advocacy from women journalists for the first time a woman has been appointed from the quota of professionals as member of the Board of Directors of state owned Radio Nepal.

New ICTs have emerged that provide opportunities to share information and resources, and link and network with each other faster. But women's presence in this new communication space still lags far behind. Access to this new medium is particularly difficult for women in poorer and less urbanised areas where telecommunications infrastructures are poor and unaffordable. Lack of skills, training and language accessibility also serves as major deterrents.

In the past few years there has been a comparatively improved and increased reportage of issues related to women in the print media. News related to women though still marginal has started to occasionally occupy important slots like the editorial, feature news, front-page news, etc. However, women's visibility in the news is still dominated by sensational stories of rape, sexual harassment, domestic violence and other forms of violence. Such portrayals have only served to reinforce rather than challenge men's suppression of women.

With increased voices and protests from active women's groups some of media's negative portrayal and representation of women have become quite subtle and insidious in the last few years. However, it is still rare that the media present women as contributors to the development process or as professionals in their own field. They are still predominantly portrayed as being victim, subservient, dependent, nurturing, selfless, sacrificing mother and wife, sex object, prostitute or mistress.

The lack of a truly gender-sensitive appreciation and analysis of women's issues by both men and women in media has allowed exploitative and derogatory images of women in media to continue. Violation of women's rights by many media still persists as is evidenced by the recent Srisha Karki incident. Srisha committed suicide unable to bear the torture inflicted on her by the media.

The Press Council is supposed to be the official monitoring body for any violation of media code of conduct but it usually addresses general media issues and has not exhibited any serious attention to improving media's portrayal and representation of women. Also there is no woman member in the Press Council.

Where earlier it was almost impossible to find a woman reporting on politics and economy now few young women have emerged who are reporting on such issues. However, the gender division of labour is still very much evident in the way coverage of stories is assigned in most media organisations. Women still tend to be assigned to "soft issues" such as culture, art, lifestyle while men are assigned to political and economic stories which are considered more as "real issues."

Although the number of women entering media is increasing, stereotyped attitudes, sexual harassment, salary differences, unfair treatment in assignments and promotions, traditional gender hierarchies, lack of support mechanisms for working women pose as obstacles that hinder women from joining the media or assuming decision-making positions. Though there has been no authentic research to justify the fact many have felt that the widespread cases of sexual harassment within media organisations has been a means to control and exclude women from occupying key positions in the industry.

The evolution of mass media in Nepal does not have a very long history. It began with the introduction of the hand press in 1851 A.D. The printing of the first monthly magazine "*Sudha Sagar*" in 1891 actually signifies the beginning of Nepali journalism. Two years later in 1901, the first weekly newspaper was published and was converted into a daily newspaper in 1960.

The first state owned "Gorkhapatra Corporation" came into being in 1964 and the first English daily "The

Rising Nepal" was brought out in 1965. The Corporation continues its publication even today. In addition to Nepali and English dailies, it also publishes one weekly paper in English and three monthly magazines in Nepali. At present, there are 8 other Nepali dailies and 3 English dailies published in the capital. There are also numerous other English and Nepali weeklies.

The restoration of multi-party democracy in Nepal in 1990 paved the way for the expansion of civil society. During the years 1950 to 1990, very few women communicators or media professionals contributed in both print and electronic media. Moreover, gender equality was not even considered an issue by the civil society and the state.

After 1990, gender and development entered into the development discourse in Nepal. The Nepali civil society began to show its great concern over the negative portrayal of women as a commodity and second class citizens through both private and government controlled print and electronic media. It is estimated that print media, both daily and weekly, presents only 7% of the total coverage on women's issues and about half of these are related to sex, prostitution, glamour, entertainment and crime. Moreover, the National Plan of Action prepared by the Ministry for Women and Social Welfare in 1997 has stated that the presence of women communicators in both electronic and print media is negligible (less than 7% in radio and print media and less than 12% in television).

The Action Plan has formulated a national policy for creating gender awareness and portraying positive images of women, increasing women's participation and developing alternate means in media. In addition to these problems within media, the whole country is facing serious gender issues such as discriminatory laws, unequal property rights, trafficking of women and girl child, lack of women's participation in public life, problems in acquiring citizenship or nationality, illiteracy, unemployment, degenerating reproductive health conditions, suffering of rural women, and violence against women and girls. These problems are perpetuated by mainstream (malestream) media.

In spite of the change in the media environment after democracy, visible improvement in terms of women's participation in the media is yet to be achieved. Of the staff working in state owned Radio Nepal, only 17% are women. Only twenty of these women are involved in mainstream journalism, mainly the news department. In Nepal Television, the percentage of women staff is 16% and in the state owned print media "The Gorkhapatra Sansthan", the national English and Nepali dailies, the percentage of women is 14%. Only three of these women are in sub editorial positions, whereas only 4% of women are employed in the National News Agency.

The private sector more or less reflects the same picture. The total percentage of women working in the media is thus estimated to be around 12%. Majority of these women occupy subordinate roles or work in the administrative sector and not in the mainstream media. Moreover, the percentage of women working in the districts is almost negligible. The trends and practices of news coverage in the state media is expected to hold much significance in making an assessment of the present situation and in contemplating the measures necessary for reinvigorating media organizations to highlight women's issues with emphasis on trafficking and other forms of violence in the future.

Radio Nepal

Radio Nepal is the only national radio station in Nepal and it is state owned. It started broadcasting in 1951 with a four-hour programme. It covers about 90% of the population by medium wave transmission through its five relay stations. Radio Nepal is able to reach places that newspapers and television are unable to reach because of the difficult topography of Nepal. Thus, radio is the most widely accessible media to the majority of the people. On Saturdays and public holidays, Radio Nepal is broadcast continuously from 5 am to 11 pm and on other days it is broadcast from 5 am to 11 am and again from 1 pm to 11 pm. Recently as a result of strong advocacy from women journalists for the first time a woman has been appointed from the quota of professionals as a member of the Board of Directors of state owned Radio Nepal.

Observing the trend of programmes on trafficking and VAW between 1st March to 14th April, 2003 it can be realized that there is minimum coverage of the issues of trafficking and other forms of violence in Radio Nepal. The monitoring of the radio programmes reveal that not much priority is accorded to issues of trafficking and other forms of violence. There is only one 15 minute weekly programme totally devoted to violence against women and trafficking and two 15 minute monthly programmes. Two of these programmes are sponsored by various organizations.

"Sachetana" is a programme totally devoted to girl trafficking which is designed to generate awareness against girl trafficking. The duration of this programme is 15 minutes and it is aired at 8:15 pm. This programme is supposed to be the only weekly programme related to trafficking but this programme is broadcast as per the priority of programmes in Radio Nepal and it is not aired every week. The programme is sponsored by Caritas Nepal.

Another monthly programme "Paridrasta" is broadcast with the objective of generating awareness against trafficking and violence against women and to provide legal advise. The duration of the programme is also 15 minutes and it is broadcast at 8:45 pm. This programme is sponsored by LACC and ABC, Nepal. Another monthly programme related to women's issues is "Barabari" which is also a 15 minute programme and this is also broadcast at 8:45 pm. This is the only non-sponsored programme that Radio Nepal has at present.

Besides the above programmes, dramas on women's issues are aired at times in the afternoons. Most of the other broadcastings related to trafficking and VAW are reporting of meetings or seminars inaugurated by prominent personalities or quoted from the various newspapers. Trafficking and VAW issues are limited to the speeches of Ministers or other dignitaries speaking at functions. Most of the other programmes give prominence to political activities. Many of the broadcasts which have been recorded are just a few sentences incorporated into other programmes.

The following strengths of Radio Nepal have been identified:

— Radio Nepal is the only form of media which reaches more than 90% of the population. § Radio Nepal can be a powerful tool for generating awareness among the people through effective programmes.

— Radio Nepal can act as a powerful tool for advocacy.

— Radio Nepal has the highest number of recipients in the kingdom.

— Compared to previous years, issues regarding trafficking and VAW have been getting some prominence.

The following weaknesses and gaps have been identified:

— At present, Radio Nepal does not have effective, regular and consistent programmes targeted towards women.

— The programmes at present are too short in duration and are aired after long intervals and the timing is not appropriate for the target audience.

— Radio Nepal gives more prominence to political activities.

— Programmes on trafficking and VAW are broadcast at a time which is not suitable for rural women.

— Lack of gender sensitivity among decision-makers.

— Lack of effective policies in order to raise gender issues.

— Lack of adequate resources for programmes on trafficking and other forms of violence.

he following analysis can be drawn from the monitoring of Radio Nepal.

— The limited programmes on trafficking and other forms of violence that are aired by Radio Nepal are inconsistent, short in duration to pass the message and aired at inappropriate timing to reach the target group.

— The programmes that are sponsored mostly air interviews of members of the same organizations and lack investigative research and in-depth reporting.

— Lack of study and lack of listener's survey.

— The news only quotes prominent people speaking at functions and lacks comments from general/local people.

— Lack of reporting of changes in policy/law and its impact in the society.

— The policy level must think in terms of increasing advocacy.

— Alongwith gender mainstreaming, there should be at least 20% focused programmes on women's issues.

The following recommendations and suggestions have been identified:

— Observing the present trend, there seems to be a need to sensitize and train the people at the decision-making level in order to give adequate priority to programmes related to trafficking and VAW.

— Development of programmes on women's issues through its own initiative instead of depending upon sponsors.

— More women would benefit if programmes related to women were broadcast at a suitable time, targeting the women in the rural areas.

— Short advertisements on VAW and trafficking at regular intervals would help generate awareness among women and girls.

— Development of effective policies to mainstream gender issues in Radio Nepal.

— Conduct a listeners survey to assess ongoing programmes and develop future programmes.

Nepal Television

Nepal Television does not have a separate policy governing the coverage of news on women, children, or people with disabilities. It is guided by the communication policy of His Majesty's Government, but in reality it is governed more by the policy undertaken by the ruling political party or parties. The government's communication policy does say that women and children's issues are a priority but in reality this is yet to be proven.

In the absence of a written policy of the state media to cover issues related to women, children, the disabled, or other vulnerable sectors of the society, the management has the discretion to decide the course of action and priority accorded to these issues. So far, Nepal Television has dictated the rules of the game in this sector alone. The other television network - Channel Nepal - is a cable television network with limited circulation, and other channels are yet to make their debut.

Looking at the gamut of NTV programmes, it is clear that they have not lived up to the expectations of the people. In the context of news coverage, NTV has given undue emphasis to portfolio news. The tendency to conduct less research and cover more scheduled news through invitations received through letters and fax has prevented the station from becoming competitive with the influx of satellite channels.

The following strengths of NTV have been identified:

— NTV is a state owned media and issues and concerns raised by it immediately draws the attention of policy makers.

— Despite its limitations, it is the best established station in Nepal accessible to the people of remote Nepal as well as Nepali expatriates via satellite, and hence its viewership is high.

— With "Communication for Development" as its motto, development issues and those concerned with women, children and other sections of the society which require more attention can be better addressed to reach the largest chunk of population through NTV.

— It is partially supported by the government which means that it need not be as profitoriented as private TV stations. As a result, the concerns of the people, including social evils such as trafficking and other forms of violence, can be discussed with emphasis, even if there are no sponsors for the programme.

Assessing the strengths and weaknesses of NTV, the following remain its shortcomings:

— As a government media it gives significant importance to minor activities of the cabinet members and the administration. It has been giving undue importance to formalities which are of no importance to other television media even if they are government-run organisations.

— There is little culture to carry out research on specific themes and bring out a revealing programme or to bring out breaking news, unless it comes naturally.

— This is blamed on limited resources and lack of interest.

— Political intervention is one of the major causes of the poor performance of NTV. Unless and until the management and staff work seriously to bring about a substantial reform in production, political intervention is less likely to subside.

The following analysis has been drawn from the monitoring of Nepal Television:

— Superficial level of reporting - lack of in-depth and follow-up reporting. § There are no regular programmes on NTV related to trafficking and violence against women - the programmes are on ad-hoc basis if and when sponsors are available.

— Women's issues are accorded low priority due to lack of adequate gender sensitivity at the decision-making level and the reporting level.

— Very few percentage of women in the decision-making level.

— Lack of integrated gender approach in all programmes.

— Women are perpetuated more as victims of various forms of violence and crime rather than professionals having their own opinion.

Despite large claims, women's issues have not been given priority as revealed by the low profile coverage of news stories and programmes. One of the major problems for this is that the news crew and production crew are not sensitized about the day to day problems that women are facing right under their nose and these problems are not focused on as important issues.

The NTV management does emphatically say that women's issues, including trafficking and violence committed against them, are prioritized. In reality however, the degree of coverage is far too little. It is clear that an understanding of the problems faced by women is discerned by only a few. It is strongly recommended that media bodies like Sancharika organize trainings and workshops for news crew and producers, to critically understand the issues that need to be given a wide coverage and understand what it means to be gender unbiased while covering the news and at all other times.

As has been observed from past experiences, NTV has not taken strong initiatives to conductresearch and carry out stories on women's issues which naturally calls for the Women Communicators Group, women activists and women organisations to organise more and more interactive programmes and workshops to apprise the media persons about the issues needing special attention from the media section.

In the one and a half month long monitoring of NTV programmes and news, the issue of women trafficking was covered only once on March 1 because an interaction programme was jointly organised by the Ministry of Women, Children and Social Welfare, UNDP and National Programme against Women Trafficking. It can be said with precision that more of such programmes would be a wake up call to media organisations.

International Women's Day comes at a fortunate time to cast light on women's issues but after the day is observed amidst a variety of functions, the coverage on women's issues sharply declines. In order to make the most of International Women's Day it is believed that women representing different professional backgrounds jointly organise a seminar to assess the effectiveness of Women's Day every year.

There is a pressing need to produce more thematic documentaries on women's issues. The copyright of the documentary could be shared between the television station and organisation which produces the documentary, increasing the possibility for television station to air the documentary during unspecified time.

A striking example is given below to illustrate the customary practice of covering hierarchical news:Gaytari mantra may be important in preserving the Vedic practices but compared to the harrowing problems that some women are facing due to prevalent socio-economic and political oppression, the importance of the Gayatri mantra could not be matched.

Trafficking and crimes on humanity such as rape make box news in newspapers but NTV hardly covers such news, neither does it dispatch its stringer reporters to go to the venue of the incident nor directs them to cover such news. NTV's disregard towards women's issues is illustrated by the fact that no news coverage has been accorded to heinous crimes against women in the past six months.

Prime time bulletin which is mostly dominated by political news. Other news bulletins cover women's issues slightly more than the prime time bulletin but the question is that prime time bulletin coverage should be far better than this. It is definitely a grim reminder of how pathetic is the coverage of women issues on the state owned Nepal Television. The coverage of Nepal television on the issue of trafficking and other social evils that women are made to bear comes down to less than 1%.

Except for the International Women's Day week, NTV coverage on women is far too negligible. The management of Nepal Television make verbal commitments that women's issues and other issues are given importance and are covered with priority. The existing pattern reveals that Nepal Television hardly assigns any reporter to conduct research stories on women's issues. News on women's issues come out only when the civil society organises workshops, seminars and public hearing programmes on the plight of women. Beyond doubt it is the weakness of Nepal Television that many acts of abuse and violence against women remain uncovered. However, women organisations could help facilitate the coverage by organising more workshops, symposiums and seminars and interaction programmes to awake broadcast stations and publication houses. The programme sector was not better in giving due importance to highlight issues and concerns of women. Documentaries based on the hardships borne by women at home and at other places were shown especially on Women's Day and the next day but it was unfortunate that the slot was not prime time. Not a single special discussion programme was organized or aired even on Women's Day.

The International Women's Day week saw a quite a lot of programmes focusing on women's issues. Except for Jagriti aired in the evening and Sankalpa aired in the afternoon, there are very few programmes that bring out women's issues. There has been a pressing need for producing new programmes to sketch the successes of women and to encourage more women to excel in their field. News based current affairs programme did not take any initiative to find women leaders to assess the status of women and to discuss the challenges lying ahead but it was the current affairs programme FOCUS in English which had Kamala Bista of SNV speaking as the Guest of the Week and sharing her thoughts on the significance of Women's Day.

Print Media

The monitoring of the print media from 1st March to 14th April 2003 reveals that the print media has given much prominence to women's issues in comparison to Radio

Nepal. A total of 17 materials related to trafficking were published in the print media. This number does not take into account the same news published by various newspapers. There were only four feature articles on trafficking and most of the publications were brief news or reporting of programmes.

There were three news reports which published the names and addresses of girls who were nearly trafficked. In the media monitoring conducted by Sancharika, it has been noticed that newspapers frequently publish the names and addresses of the victims of trafficking which generally tends to further victimize such victims. Regarding activities, a total of 9 interaction programmes, workshops, discussion programmes, rally and anniversary was reported by the media. Among these, the Ministry of Women, Children and Social Welfare (MOWCSW), UNDP Task Force and Joint Initiatives against Trafficking (JIT) were the major implementers of the programmes.

Regarding violence against women, a total of 62 news articles were published relating to witch accusation and domestic violence during the period. Among these, three news related publications were given priority as anchor news on the first page. Approximately 19 women were reported to have died due to some form of violence during the period. A total of 9 articles related to VAW were published by the media. Most of the other reportings were brief news of incidents of violence. There were only two interaction programmes slightly related to VAW reported by the media. One was on discriminatory laws and its impact on women and the other was on the role of the civil society regarding women and children victims of armed conflict.

The following conclusions can be drawn from the above media trend:

— There was much less reporting on both trafficking and VAW during the period.

— The trend to publish names and addresses of victims of trafficking still exists.

— There were very few programmes implemented during the period. § The media has not given much priority to providing space to articles related to women's issues.

Other forms of violence such as rape, witch accusation, and women in armed conflict were also reported by the media. The media also published news of various workshops, seminars and programmes related to trafficking and VAW implemented by various organizations. A large number of organizations celebrated March 8th as the "93rd International Women's Day" and the media gave much coverage to the functions. Also, a large number of articles and editorials were published to mark the day. The other highlight during the period was articles and editorials published on the role of women in the peace process and the plight of widows due to the Maoist conflict.

Many articles were also published on women's health, especially on the complications after abortion. Although only a few of these publications were given priority on the first page, the number of materials that were published shows that there has been an increase in reporting on womenrelated issues in comparison to the past.

The following strengths of the print media have been identified:

— Effective in raising awareness instantly among the general public.

— A very effective tool for advocacy at the policy level.

— Easy to maintain records for monitoring and evaluation.

The print media has definitely improved in their reporting of women's issues in comparison to the past. The following analysis has been drawn from the monitoring during the period:

— There is still a need for gender sensitization among reporters.

— In most cases, one reporter is assigned to various issues which may create confusion due to lack of clarity and knowledge of the particular subject. It is best to assign a particular reporter to a certain beat.

— Training and capacity building of reporters needs to be enhanced.

— Most of the media organizations are poorly equipped and have minimum facilities. INGOs and NGOs can support the reporters by providing information through their own channels.

The following recommendations and suggestions have been identified for print media:

— A need to generate awareness and sensitize the people at the decision-making level (editors, chief editors, etc.,) and the journalists.

— Encourage the involvement of women in decision-making at all levels and achieve gender balance in the appointment of women.

— Develop effective policies and implement programmes including educational programmes, on changing stereotypical attitude and behaviours concerning women's issues.

— Strengthen efforts to fully implement national action plans developed for the implementation of the Beijing Platform of Action and when necessary adjust or develop national plans for the future.

— Provide national machinery with the necessary human and financial resources including through exploring innovative funding schemes so that women's issues are integrated in all policies, programs and projects.

5

Media and Violence

For decades, media writers, directors and producers have been trying to tell us that the violent content of the media they create also doesn't hurt, that is, that despite its glamour and impact, it plays no role in making this a more violent society. They may have had a case earlier in this century when portrayals of media violence were less believable but today the proliferation of realistic-looking mayhem, assualt and death makes for a totally different situation. According to opinion of one expert, of the 25,000 murders committed in the United States every year, at least half are due to the influence and desensitizing effects of media violence. At minimum, media violence may be most influential in modeling the use of deadly force as the primary, if not the only, way to solve problems and resolve interpersonal conflict.

Many blame media for the rise in violence, but of course that's not the whole story. It's also clear that overcrowding, pervasive life-long poverty, hunger, joblessness and drug addiction — as well as the ready availability of guns —also contribute to our skyrocketing homicide rate. But the media connection can no longer be ignored.

Never before has journalism and have journalists been under such intense scrutiny as they are today. The media are a "hot topic" and getting a lot hotter. The reason is really fairly simple. It's because life has become so complicated--our politics, our economy, our social environment have all become so complex, so interrelated, that it's hard for the citizen to make head or tail of what's going on. So the media's role is to provide the agenda of the day's happenings—the news most important and most relevant to you—the details, the significance, the background. Its role is to not only chronicle the past and the present, but to signal the future, to look for trends and implications. Whether they read about what's happening in the newspapers, hear it on radio or see it on television, journalism is basically how members of a modern democratic society keep in touch. It's the prime, cohesive factor in creating, nourishing, adjusting and sustaining a democratic society.

Our journalism today is hasty. It's incomplete, sometimes inaccurate, occasionally misleading. The media are imperfect, but they are also an absolute necessity. Journalism—this imperfect necessity—is the hinge of democracy. It is the only way we are going to find out about the events and issues that dominate our lives. Without journalism, there would be a universal sense of uncertainty because people simply wouldn't know what was going on. The basic points are:

— the media are the adhesive that holds together a democratic society.

— although under increasing criticism,

— the media are doing a better job today than ever before.

There are all kinds of power centres in any democracy: the judiciary, the government mandarins, the elected representatives, the establishment, the business community, the unions. What binds it all together is the media. Only through the media can the governing communicate with the governed in any mass sense.

A real, participatory democracy today simply can't survive without a free, independent and professionally- and socially-responsible media. And it is precisely because of that critical role of the media that society's leaders try to manipulate the media. They want to shape our reporting to their objective. Prime ministers, presidents, all political leaders, view managing the media as a vital precondition to their domination of the legislature or the Parliament, the public and the whole political process.

Increasingly, corporate executives, labour leaders and social activists of all kinds, are taking the same view and seeking to manipulate the news so that their point of view dominates headlines, not somebody else's. That is why the new business of "Spin Doctors" is thriving. The 'Spin Doctors' in politics and elsewhere are usually very nice, friendly public-relations people whose job is to make a cabbage smell like a rose. They want to have the media reflect their own self-image. They prefer a sympathetic and sometimes sycophantic media, not an assertively-independent media. Now that is understandable, but sympathy and sycophancy are not in our job specs in the media. Our role is fundamentally different. Our role is to try to reflect reality, not somebody's self-image. The media is essentially a teacher in the broadest sense of that word. The media must be assertively independent, insatiably curious and maybe we are demanding. But we are, because the media are, in effect, agents for the public in trying to provide that fair reflection of reality in seeking out and providing information on what's happening, where, when and why. These days, reporters do hear such a lot of manipulative rhetoric—so many statements that seem to be promises chiselled in water, especially among our political leaders.

People complain that the media spend too much time reporting bad news. In fact, people have been complaining about that for centuries. Sophocles once declared that, "Nobody likes the man who brings bad news." Well, nobody does, and it's true, we do report a lot of bad news. But that's because there is a lot of bad news in this world of ours. To pretend it isn't there, to be some kind of emotional cheer leader, is to fail as a journalist. Our responsibility to the public is to try to present reality, not wishful thinking. Our challenge is to strive relentlessly to come as close as we possibly can to providing that reality so people can understand and can cope with the real world around them. Politicians, business people, labour and social activists have to realize that disputing reality will never change reality. And a key part of our journalistic job is to enlarge public understanding of what for some may be uncomfortable facts.

The media's role is to provide the raw material for the public dialogue. And that means the media have an enormous responsibility because a nation's vibrancy and confidence depends on its awareness of what's happening, what's changing.

There are lot of criticism agianst journalists and they are often accused of having delusions of adequacy. But most journalists are not trying to shoot the wounded. What they are trying to do is to sift through the rhetoric of society's leaders and would-be leaders, to try to find reality. Too often, though, people in both the public and private sectors, are not so much interested in reality as they are in perception.

If we steer our lives and our country on perceptions only, then at some point we're going to have some very rude shocks when we come face to face with reality. There simply has to be room in a democratic society for things you may not like to hear there has to be freedom for the thought you may hate.

Media's Influence on Children

The child and the media" is the theme for the next general discussion of the United Nations Committee on the Rights of the Child. The discussion will take place on 7 October 1996 at the United Nations Office at Geneva. United Nations bodies and specialized agencies as well as non-governmental organizations and representatives of the media, including organizations of journalists, are invited to take part in this full-day discussion. This decision was taken by the Committee on the Rights of the Child at its eleventh session in the light of rule 75 of the its provisional rules of procedure. The purpose of the general discussions is to enhance a deeper understanding of the content and implications of the Convention. The discussions are public.

The Convention on the Rights of the Child is formally addressed to Governments and does not interfere with the independence of the media; however, it does have an indirect message for media institutions: as with human rights in general, the press and other media have essential functions in promoting and protecting the fundamental rights of the child. The Committee on the Rights of the Child believes that the media - both written and audiovisual - are highly important in the efforts to make reality the principles and standards of the Convention.

The media in many countries have already contributed greatly in creating an awareness of the Convention and its content. The media could also play a pivotal role in monitoring the actual implementation of the rights of the child. In their reporting the media give an "image" of the child; they reflect and influence perceptions about who children are and how they behave. This image could create and convey respect for young people; however, it could also spread prejudices and stereotypes which may have a negative influence on public opinion and politicians. Nuanced and well-informed reporting is to the benefit of the rights of the child.

It is important that the media themselves do not abuse children. The integrity of the child should be protected in reporting about, for instance, involvement in criminal activities, sexual abuse and family problems. Fortunately, the media in some countries have voluntarily agreed to respect guidelines which offer such protection of the privacy of the child; however, such ethical standards are not always adhered to.

Concern has also been expressed about the influence on children of negative aspects of the media, primarily programmes containing brutal violence and pornography. There is discussion in a number of countries about how to protect children from violence on television in video films and in other modern media. Again, voluntary agreements have been attempted, with varied impact. This particular problem is raised in article 17 of the Convention which recommends that appropriate guidelines be developed "for the protection of the child from information and material injurious to his or her well-being". Such guidelines have indeed been developed in some countries, with varied results. The United Nations Educational, Scientific and Cultural Organization has recently renewed discussion on this topic.

The media is important for offering children the possibility of expressing themselves. One of the principles of the Convention is that the views of children be heard and given due respect. This is also reflected in articles about freedom of expression, thought, conscience and religion. It is in the spirit of these provisions that children should not only be able to consume information material but also to participate themselves in the media. This requires that there exist media which communicate with children.

The Committee on the Rights of the Child has noted that there have been experiments in several countries to develop child-oriented media; some daily newspapers have special pages for children and radio and television programmes also devote special segments for the young audience. Further efforts are, however, needed.

Role of Communication in Preventing Crime

The field of communication for social change (CSC) covers a variety of concepts and strategies such as: communications for development, development communications, social marketing, "edutainment", "infotainment" or enter-educate, participatory communication, etc. In recent years, several international meetings and events have taken place to bring together communication professionals, community organizers,

NGO's, practitioners, social change activists, broadcasters, and funders to help define the field, investigate theoretical frameworks, discuss new developments, and suggest new ways forward in the field. The most notable are:

1) The Communication and Social Change: Forging Strategies for a New Century Conference, Bellagio, Italy, April 1997. Sponsored by the Rockefeller Foundation. A series of action steps was agreed upon including: to convince others of the value of the CSC approach, to publicise writings about its effectiveness, and to continue to study prospects in the global community (Rockefeller Foundation 2001, p.8). Follow-up meetings were held in Cape Town, South Africa in 1998 and 2000. Following from the 1998 Cape Town meeting, the Rockefeller Foundation developed a concrete definition of Communication for Social Change: A process of public and private dialogue through which people define who they are, what they want and how they can get it. In addition, this event led to an outline of the skills and attributes needed to do work in the field, preliminary work on a practitioner's toolkit, an agreement in measurement, and the establishment of several linking networks.

2) The Third International Entertainment Education Conference for Social Change, Arnhem and Amsterdam, The Netherlands, 2000 hosted by the Netherlands Entertainment-Education Foundation in collaboration with Johns Hopkins University Centre for Communication Programs. This event led to the adoption of the Entertainment Education (EE) declaration outlining seven vital positions for the sustainability of EE and sets out future work in the area. These are:

a) The synergy of entertainment and education consists of deliberately combining the joy of entertainment with the empowering potential of education to achieve social progress for all.

b) Ethics in the field of Entertainment-Education should encourage full and informed participation of all stakeholders, especially including audiences. Ethical practice is based on appropriate information and includes careful design and monitoring of implementation processes as well as societal consequences of Entertainment -Education.

c) Theory and practice are based on inclusiveness, diversity, and a variety of genres, multidisciplinary theories, methods, formats and channels. Theory and practice incorporate intuitive and scientific modern and traditional approaches, including folk media, community broadcasting and emerging technologies. Theory and practice facilitate transcreational and locally adaptable formats, applicable to individuals and communities.

d) We recognize the importance of conducting and sharing research to the development of the Entertainment-Education field. We encourage fine-tuning of current research methods and support new and more comprehensive approaches for formative, monitoring and evaluation. We will set a research agenda that includes study into the role of performing artists, their involvement in social subjects, and intended and unintended effects.

e) We will expand professional expertise through continuing pre-service and in-service training and education in related professional fields as well as the Entertainment -Education sector through academic and on-the-job training methods.

f) Entertainment-Education promotes sound business practices that will support sustainability, including branding and marketing, to optimize cost-effectiveness with a fair and equitable financial return to all participants.

g) We agree to develop a network of associates that will facilitate the exchange of information and materials and that will function as an advocate for Entertainment-Education. The three organizing parties of this event here commit to sustaining this network, establishing and coordinating a Web site developing a global distribution system for existing Entertainment-Education materials, and other initiatives. We will plan for future meetings amongst our organisations and with other interested parties; and establish awards to recognize excellence in the Entertainment - Education field.

3) *The Competencies:* Communication for Development and Social Change conference held at Rockefeller Foundation, Bellagio, Italy, January 28 - February 1, 2002. This led to the publication "Mapping Competencies for Development and Social Change: Turning Knowledge, Skills and Attitudes into Action," released in November 2002.

4) *The IV International Conference on Communication* : Perspectives on Communication for Social Change3, May 2003. Organized by the Universidad de Norte with the support of the Communication Initiative Latin America (CILA).This event provided an

opportunity for academics, activists, experts and thinkers to reflect critically on the topic of communication for social change.

5) Communication for Social Change Forum, Ottawa Canada, May 2003. Hosted by South Asian Partnership Canada (SAP) and funded by Canadian International Development Agency (CIDA), this event gathered academics, NGOs, development consultants, government officials and communication officers from 15 countries. Topics covered included: Definition of Communication for Social Change, Traditional Examples of CSC (eg. interactive theatre), Information Communication Technologies and Challenges and Possibilities. The most recent definition of CSC follows from this event.

It is defined as a process whereby internal or external groups intentionally send messages through various communication mediums into a targeted community or society with the intention that their message will be properly ingested to produce a change in behavior or action. The main underlying assumption of CSC work is that we can find effective ways to use the field of communication to make greater contributions to the pace of development.

Principles and Objectives

To inform the identification and selection of good practice in the field, the Rockefeller Foundation has identified the following principles of CSC:

— it empowers individuals and communities

— it engages people in making decisions that enhance their lives

— it focuses on direct and many-to-many communications

— it relies on democratic ideals

— it allows previously unheard voices to be heard, and

— both the process of communications and the content of the messages are controlled by the receiving communities

While partners involved in a CSC initiative may have different objectives some of the main objectives of the CSC process areto:

— inform, initiate and encourage people to engage in collective action;

— help people make better decisions for themselves;

— change specific behaviour where appropriate; and

— promote equitable access to resources and services.

Challenges

Similar to communication practitioners in general, and crime prevention practitioners in particular, CSC practitioners encounter the following challenges:

— *Assessing Impact*: How to measure effectiveness beyond counting products produced (eg. number of messages disseminated) or net impressions received (eg. audience ratings). Other issues related to participatory evaluation are discussed in "Making Waves: Stories of participatory communication for social change".

— *Making Strategic links*: How to program communication for social change work on the micro community level and on the multinational level, often simultaneously.

— *Knowledge Transfer*: How to transfer information, skills, tools, resources and training to those most in need and those who live in hard-to reach areas.

— *Language:* How to ensure that the CSC philosophy and methodology is readily accessible to a wider audience (e.g. beyond communication practitioners).

— *Learning by Cases*: Sharing Stories: How to ensure that case studies selected are those which capture the imagination of audiences and communities, yet are not overly simplistic.

A number of concerns and areas of disagreement can be identified in the field of communication for social change. Some are related to long-term standing issues in development work in general. Others are more recent, but in all cases they can help to inform and expand current thinking about the role of communication in crime prevention and community safety. They include concerns about:

— the extent to which beneficiaries are consulted throughout all stages of the development and implementation of community safety initiatives

— the extent to which the cultural values of different community groups are considered in diagnosis, implementation, monitoring and evaluation stages.

— the over-emphasis on internet-based tools for social change verses other mediums such as community radio, video, theatre, puppets, etc. These is especially important given the high illiteracy rates in developing countries

— the lack of access to Information Communication Technologies (ICT's), though it is not clear if this access will contribute to social change or act as fashionable gadget.

— the donors' need for short-term results: the requirement of proving "success' in the short term while excluding qualitative issues, and long term benefits.

Despite these problems and areas of disagreement, there is compelling evidence to suggest that communication can wield great power in development. Moreover, while not a 'cure-all', communication for social change can contribute to improving the quality of life of citizens by establishing a dialogue with citizens throughout all stages of policy interventions. Indeed, the crime prevention field has much to gain from moving beyond its traditional communication strategies and initiatives and recognizing communication as a full partner, rather than an "add on" to the crime prevention process.

6

Strategies of Developmental Communication

Development communication commonly refers to the application of communication strategies and principles in the developing world. It has its origins in post-war international aid programs to countries in Latin America, Asia and Africa that were struggling with poverty, illiteracy, poor health and a lack of economic, political and social infrastructures. It is derived from theories of development and social change that identified the main problems of the post-war world in terms of a lack of development or progress equivalent to Western countries.

Development theories have their roots in mid-century optimism about the prospects that large parts of the post-colonial world could eventually "catch-up" and resemble Western countries. After the last remains of European empires in Africa and Asia crumbled in the 1950s and 1960s, a dominant question in policy and academic quarters was how to address the abysmal disparities between the developed and underdeveloped worlds. Development originally meant the process by which Third

World societies could become more like Western developed societies as measured in terms of political system, economic growth, and educational levels. Development was synonymous with political democracy, rising levels of productivity and industrialization, high literacy rates, longer life expectancy, and the like. The implicit assumption was that there was one form of development as expressed in developed countries that underdeveloped societies needed to replicate. Since then, numerous studies have provided diverse definitions of development communication.

Definitions reflect different scientific premises of researchers as well as interests and political agendas of a myriad of foundations and organizations in the development field. Recent definitions state that the ultimate goal of "development communication" is to raise the quality of life of populations, including increase income and well-being, eradicate social injustice, promote land reform and freedom of speech, and establish community centers for leisure and entertainment. The current aim of development communication is to remove constraints for a more equal and participatory society.Although a multiplicity of theories and concepts emerged during the past fifty years, studies and interventions have fundamentally offered two different diagnoses and answers to the problem of underdevelopment. While one position has argued that the problem was largely due to lack of information among populations, the other one suggested that power inequality was the underlying problem. Because the diagnoses were different, recommendations were different, too. Running the risk of overgeneralization, it could be said that theories and intervention approaches fell in different camps on the following points:

- — Cultural vs. environmental explanations for underdevelopment.
- — Psychological vs. socio-political theories and interventions.
- — Attitudinal and behavior models vs. structural and social models.
- — Individual vs. community-centered interventions development.
- — Hierarchical and sender-oriented vs. horizontal and participatory communication models.
- — Active vs. passive conceptions of audiences and populations.
- — Participation as means vs. participation as end approaches.

These divergences are explored in the examination of theories and approaches below.

Dominant Paradigm in the Field of Development Communication

Behavior change models have been the dominant paradigm in the field of development communication. Different theories and strategies shared the premise that problems of development were basically rooted in lack of knowledge and that, consequently, interventions needed to provide people with information to change behavior. The early generation of development communication studies was dominated by modernization theory. This theory suggested that cultural and information deficits lie underneath development problems, and therefore could not be resolved only through economic assistance. Instead, the difficulties in Third World countries were at least partially related to the existence of a traditional culture that inhibited development.

Third World countries lacked the necessary culture to move into a modern stage. Culture was viewed as the "bottleneck" that prevented the adoption of modern attitudes and behavior. McClelland and Hagen, for example, understood that personalities determined social structure. Traditional personalities, characterized by authoritarianism, low self-esteem, and resistance to innovation, were diametrically different from modern personalities and, consequently, anti-development. These studies best illustrated one of modernization's central tenets: ideas are the independent variable that explains specific outcomes.

Based on this diagnosis, development communication proposed that changes in ideas would result in transformations in behavior. The underlying premise, originated in classic sociological theories, was that there is a necessary fitness between a "modern" culture and economic and political development. The low rate of agricultural output, the high rate of fertility and mortality, or the low rates of literacy found in the underdeveloped world were explained by the persistence of traditional values and attitudes that prevented modernization. The goal was, therefore, to instill modern values and information through the transfer of media technology and the adoption of innovations and culture originated in the developed world. The Western model of development was upheld as the model to be emulated worldwide.

Because the problem of underdeveloped regions was believed to be an information problem, communication was presented as the instrument that would solve it. As theorized by Daniel Lerner and Wilbur Schramm, communication basically meant the transmission of information. Exposure to mass media was one of the factors among others (e.g. urbanization, literacy) that could bring about modern attitudes. This knowledge-transfer model defined the field for years to come. Both Lerner's and Schramm's analyses and recommendations had a clear pro-media, pro-innovation, and pro-persuasion focus. The emphasis was put on media-centered persuasion activities that could improve literacy and, in turn, allow populations to break free from traditionalism.

This view of change originated in two communication models. One was the Shannon-Weaver model of sender-receiver, originally developed in engineering studies that set out to explain the transmission of information among machines. It became extremely influential in communication studies. The other was the propaganda model developed during World War II according to which the mass media had "magic bullet" effects in changing attitudes and behavior.

From a transmission/persuasion perspective, communication was understood as a linear, unidirectional process in which senders send information through media channels to receivers. Consequently, development communication was equated with the massive introduction of media technologies to promote modernization, and the widespread adoption of the mass media (newspapers, radio, cinemas, and later television) was seen as pivotal for the effectiveness of communication interventions.

The media were both channels and indicators of modernization: they would serve as the agents of diffusion of modern culture, and also, suggested the degree of modernization of society. The emphasis on the diffusion of media technologies meant that modernization could be measured and quantified in terms of media penetration. The numbers of television and radio sets and newspaper consumption were accepted as indicators of modern attitudes. Statistics produced by the United Nations Educational, Scientific and Cultural Organization (UNESCO) showing the penetration of newspapers, radio and television sets became proxy of development.

Researchers found that in countries where people were more exposed to modern media, more favorable attitudes towards modernization and development. Based on these findings, national governments and specialists agreed to champion the media as instruments for the dissemination of modern ideas that would improve agriculture, health, education, and politics. So-called "small" media such as publications, posters and leaflets were also recommended as crucial to the success of what became known as Development Support Communication, that is, the creation of the human environment necessary for a development program to succeed".

The "diffusion of innovations" theory elaborated by Everett Rogers became one of the most influential modernization theories. It has been said that Rogers' model has ruled development communication for decades and became the blueprint for communication activities in development. Rogers' intention was to understand the adoption of new behaviors. The premise was that innovations diffuse over time according to individuals' stages.

Having reviewed over 500 empirical studies in the early 1960s, Rogers posited five stages through which an individual passes in the adoption of innovations: awareness, knowledge and interest, decision, trial, and adoption/rejection. Populations were divided in different groups according to their propensity to incorporate innovations and timing in actually adopting them.

Rogers proposed that early adopters act as models to emulate and generate a climate of acceptance and an appetite for change, and those who are slow to adopt are laggards. This latter category was assumed to describe the vast majority of the population in the Third World. For Rogers, the subculture of the peasantry offered important psychological constraints on the incorporation of innovations, and consequently, development. His view on development reflected the transmission bias also found in Lerner and Schramm.

According to Rogers, development communications entailed a "process by which an idea is transferred from a source to a receiver with the intent to change his behavior. Usually the source wants to alter the receiver's knowledge of some idea, create or change his attitude toward the idea, or persuade him to adopt the idea as part of his regular behavior" However, diverging from the media-centrism and "magic bullet" theory of effects that underpinned earlier analyses, Rogers and subsequent "diffusion" studies concluded that the media had a great importance in increasing awareness but that interpersonal communication and personal sources were crucial in making decisions to adopt innovations.

This revision incorporated insights from the opinion leader theory according to which there are two steps in information flow: from the media to opinion leaders, and from leaders to the masses. Media audiences rely on the opinions of members of their social networks rather solely or mainly on the mass media. In contrast to powerful media effects models that suggested a direct relation between the mass media and the masses, Lazarsfeld and Katz found that interpersonal relations were crucial in channeling and shaping opinion.

This insight was incorporated in diffusion studies, which proposed that both exposure to mass media and face-to-face interaction were necessary to induce effective change. The effectiveness of field workers in transmitting information in agricultural development projects also suggested the importance of interpersonal networks in disseminating innovations. Consequently, a triadic model of communication was recommended that included change agents, beneficiaries, and communicators.

Confirming Lerner's and Schramm's ideas, another important finding of diffusion research was that what motivates change is not economics but communication and culture. This is what studies on how farmers adopted new methods showed. Such studies were particularly influential because a substantial amount of early efforts targeted agricultural development in the Third World.

Other applications targeted literacy programs and health issues, mainly family planning and nutrition. In the mid-1970s, main representatives of modernization/ diffusion theories considered it necessary to review some basic premises. In a widely quoted article, Rogers admitted "the passing of the dominant paradigm." Schramm and Rogers recognized that early views had individualistic and psychological biases. It was necessary to be sensitive to the specific sociocultural environment in which "communication" took place, an issue that was neglected in early analyses. To a large extent, these revisions resulted from the realization that the "trickle down" model that was originally championed was not proven to be effective in instrumenting change. The stages model remained but the top-down perspective according to which innovations diffuse from above needed modification.

Other positions suggested that the traditional model needed to integrate a process orientation that was not only focussed on the results of intervention but also to pay attention to content, and address the cognitive dimensions (not just behavior). Many of these observations were integrated into the diffusion approach. By the mid-1970s, Rogers' definition of communication showed important changes that partially responded to criticisms.

Development was theorized as a participatory process of social change intended to bring social and material advancement. Communication was no longer focussed on persuasion (transmission of information between individuals and groups), but was understood as a "process by which participants create and share information with one another in order to reach a mutual understanding".

Theories in the Dominant Paradigm Tradition

In the early 1970s, modernization theory was the dominant paradigm of development communication. The climate of enthusiasm and "missionary zeal," as Wilbur Schramm described it, that had existed a decade earlier had notably receded but the notion that the diffusion of information and innovations could solve problems of under-development prevailed.

Social Marketing Approach

Social marketing has been one of the approaches that has carried forward the premises of diffusion of innovation and behavior change models. Since the 1970s, social marketing has been one of the most influential strategies in the field of development communication. The origins of social marketing hark back to the intention of marketing to expand its disciplinary boundaries. It was clearly a product of specific political and academic developments in the United States that were later incorporated into development projects.

Among various reasons, the emergence of social marketing responded to two main developments: the political climate in the late 1960s that put pressure on various disciplines to attend to social issues, and the emergence of nonprofit organizations that found marketing to be a useful tool.

Social marketing was marketing's response to the need to be "socially relevant" and "socially responsible." It was a reaction of marketing as both discipline and industry to be sensitive to social issues and to strive towards the social good. But it was also a way for marketing to provide intervention tools to organizations whose business was the promotion of social change.

Social marketing consisted of putting into practice standard techniques in commercial marketing to promote pro-social behavior. From marketing and advertising, it imported theories of consumer behavior into the development communication. The analysis of consumer behavior required to understand the complexities, conflicts and influences that cretae consumer needs and how needs can be met. Influences include environmental, invididual, and information processing and decision making. At the core of social marketing theory is the exchange model according to which individuals, groups and organizations exchange resources for perceived benefits of purchasing products. The aim of interventions is to create voluntary exchanges.

In terms of its place on the "family tree" of development communication, social marketing did not come out of either diffusion or participatory theories, the traditions that dominated the field in the early 1970s. Social marketing was imported from a discipline that until then had little to do with modernization or dependency theories, the thendominant approaches in development communication. Social marketing grew out of the disciplines of advertising and marketing in the United States. The central premise of these disciplines underlies social marketing strategies: the goal of an advertising/ marketing campaign is to make the public aware about the existence, the price, and the benefits of specific products.

Social marketing's focus on behavior change, understanding of communication as persuasion ("transmission of information"), and top-down approach to instrument change suggested an affinity with modernization and diffusion of innovation theories. Similar to diffusion theory, it conceptually subscribed to a sequential model of behavior change in which individuals cognitively move from acquisition of knowledge to adjustment of attitudes toward behavior change. However, it was not a natural extension of studies in development communication.

What social marketing brought was a focus on using marketing techniques such as market segmentation and formative research to maximize the effectiveness of interventions. The use of techniques from commercial advertising and marketing to promote social/political goals in international issues was not new in the 1970s. Leading advertising agencies and public relations firms had already participated in support of U.S. international policies, most notably during the two wars in drumming up domestic approval and mobilization for war efforts. Such techniques, however, had not been used before to "sell" social programs and goals worldwide.

One of the standard definitions of social marketing states that "it is the design, implementation, and control of programs calculated to influence the acceptability of social ideas and involving consideration of product planning, pricing, communication, distribution, and marketing research". More recently, Andreasen has defined it as "the adaptation of commercial marketing technologies to programs designed to influence the voluntary behavior of target audiences to improve their personal welfare and that of the society of which they are a part." Others have defined it as the application of management and marketing technologies to pro-social and nonprofit programs.

Social marketing suggested that the emphasis should be put not so much on getting ideas out or transforming attitudes but influencing behavior. For some of its best-known proponents, behavior change is social marketing's bottom line, the goal that sets it apart from education or propaganda. Unlike commercial marketing, which is not concerned with the social consequences of its actions, the social marketing model centers on communication campaigns designed to promote socially beneficial practices or products in a target group.

Social marketing's goal is to position a product such as condoms by giving information that could help fulfill, rather than create, uncovered demand. It intends to "reduce the psychological, social, economic and practical distance between the consumer and the behavior". The goal would be to make condom-use affordable, available and atractive. If couples of reproductive age do not want more children but do not use any contraceptive, the task of social marketing is to find out why and what information needs to be provided so they can make informed choices. This requires sorting out cultural beliefs that account for such behavior or for why people are unwilling to engage in certain health practices even when they are informed about their positive results. This knowledge is the baseline that allows a successful positioning of a product. A product needs to be positioned in the context of community beliefs.

In the United States, social marketing has been extensively applied in public information campaigns that targeted a diversity of problems such as smoking, alcoholism, seat-belt use, drug abuse, eating habits, venereal diseases, littering and protection of forests. The Stanford Three-Community Study of Heart Disease is frequently mentioned as one of the most fully documented applications of the use of marketing strategies.

Designed and implemented as a strictly controlled experiment, it offered evidence that it is possible to change behavior through the use of marketing methodologies. The campaign included television spots, television programming, radio spots, newspaper advertisements and stories, billboard messages and direct mail. In one town the media campaign was supplemented by interpersonal communication with a random group of individuals at risk of acquiring heart disease. Comparing results among control and experimental communities, the research concluded that media could be a powerful inducer of change, especially when aligned with the interpersonal activities of community groups.

Social marketing has been used in developing countries in many interventions such as condom use, breast-feeding, and immunization programs. According to

Chapman Walsh and associates, "early health applications of social marketing emerged as part of the international development efforts and were implemented in the third world during the 1960s and 1970s. Programs promoting immunization, family planning, various agricultural reforms, and nutrition were conducted in numerous countries in Africa, Asia and South America during the 1970s...The first nationwide contraceptive program social marketing program, the Nirodh condom project in India, began in 1967 with funding from the Ford Foundation."

The substantial increase in condom sales was attributed to the distribution and promotion of condoms at a subsidized price. The success of the Indian experience informed subsequent social marketing interventions such as the distribution of infant-weaning formula in public health clinics.

According to Fox N.D., "problems arose with the social marketing approach, however, over the motives of their sponsors, the effectiveness of their applications, and, ultimately, the validity of their results. The social marketing of powdered milk products, replacing or supplementing breastfeeding in the third world, provides an example of these problems.

In the 1960's multinational firms selling infant formulas moved into the virgin markets of Asia, Africa and Latin America. Booklets, mass media, loudspeaker vans, and distribution through the medical profession were used in successful promotion campaigns to switch traditional breastfeeding to artificial products. Poor people, however, could not afford such products, and many mothers diluted the formula to make it last longer or were unable to properly sterilize the water or bottle. The promotion of breast milk substitutes often resulted in an erosion of breastfeeding and led to increases in diarrheal diseases and malnutrition, contributing to the high levels of infant mortality in the third world."

Critics have lambasted social marketing for manipulating populations and being solelyconcerned with goals without regard for means. For much of its concerns about ethics, critics argue, social marketing subscribes to a utilitarian ethical model that prioritizes ends over means. In the name of achieving certain goals, social marketing justifies any methods. Like marketing, social marketing deceives and manipulates people into certain behaviors.

Social marketers have responded by arguing that campaigns inform publics and that they use methods that are not intrinsically good or bad. Judgments should be contingent on what goals they are meant to serve, they argue. Moreover, the widely held belief that marketing has the ability to trick and make people do what otherwise they would not is misinformed and incorrect.

The reluctance of people to tailor behavior to the recommendations of social marketing campaigns, and the fact that campaigns need to be adjusted to socio-cultural contexts and morals are evidence that social marketing lacks the much-attributed power of manipulating audiences. If a product goes against traditional beliefs and behavior, campaigns are likely to fail. Social marketing needs to be consumer oriented, and knowledgeable of the belief systems and the communication channels used in a community. Products need to be marketed according to the preferences and habits of customers.

Market research is necessary because it provides development specialists with tools to know consumers better and, therefore, to prevent potential problems and pitfalls in behavior change. This is precisely marketing's main contribution: systematic, reasearch-based information about consumers that is indiuspensable for the success of interventions.

Marketing research techniques are valuable for finding out thoughts and attitudes about a given issue that help prevent possible failures and position a product. For its advocates, one of the main strengths of social marketing is that it allows to position products and concepts in traditional belief systems. The inclination of many programs to forgo in-depth research of targeted populations for funding or time considerations, social marketers suggest, reflects the lack of understanding about the need to have basic research to plan, execute and evaluate interventions. They argue that social marketing cannot manipulate populations by positioning a product with false appeals to local beliefs and practices.

If the desired behavior is not present in the local population, social marketing cannot deceive by wrapping the product with existing beliefs. When a product is intended to have effects that are not present in the target population, social marketers cannot provide false information that may resonate with local belief systems but, instead, need to provide truthful information about its consequences. For example, if "dehydration" does not exist as a health concept in the community, it would be ethically wrong for social marketing to position a dehydration product by falsely appealing to existing health beliefs in order to sell it. That would be deceptive and manipulative and is sure to backfire. The goal should be long-term health benefits rather than the short-term goals of a given campaign.

Theorists and practitioners identified with participatory communication have been strong critics of social marketing. For them, social marketing is a non-participatory strategy because it treats most people as consumers rather than protagonists. Because it borrows techniques from Western advertising, it shares it premises, namely, a concern with selling products rather than participation.

To critics, social marketing is concerned with individuals, not with groups or organizations. They also view social marketing as an approach that intends to persuade people to engage in certain behaviors that have already decided by agencies and planners. It does not involve communities in deciding problems and courses of action. The goal should be, instead, to assist populations in changing their actions based on critical analysis of social reality.

According to participatory approaches, change does not happen when communities are not actively engaged in development projects and lack a sense of ownership. Social marketers have brushed aside these criticisms, emphasizing that social marketing is a two-way process and that it is genuinely concerned about community participation.

As Novelli puts it, "the marketing process is circular." This is why input from targeted communities, gathered through qualitative methods such as focus groups and in-depth interviews, is fundamental to design campaign activities and content. Social marketing is premised on the idea of mutual exchange between agencies and communities. Marketing takes a consumer orientation by assuming that the success of any intervention results from an accurate evaluation of perceptions, needs, and wants of target markets that inform the design, communication, pricing, and delivery of appropriate offerings.

The process is consumer-driven, not expert-driven. Also, social marketing allows communities to participate by acting upon health, environmental and other problems. Without information, there is no participation and this is what social marketing offers. Such participation is voluntary: Individuals, groups, and organizations are not forced to participate but are offered the opportunity to gain certain benefits. Such explanation is not satisfactory to participatory communication advocates who respond that social marketing does not truly involve participation. More than a narrow conception of participation, they argue, social marketing offers the appearance of it to improve interventions that are centralized.

Social marketing's conception of participation basically conceives campaigns' targets are "passive receivers," subjects from whom information is obtained to change products and concepts. After three decades of research and interventions, the lessons of social marketing can be summarized as follows:

— Persistence and a long-term perspective are essential. Only programs with sustainable support and commitment have proven to have impact on diffusion of new ideas and practices, particularly in cases of complex behavior patterns.

— Segmentation of the audience is central. Some researchers have identified different lifestyle clusters that allow a better identification of different market niches.

— Mapping target groups is necessary. Designers of interventions need to know where potential consumers live, their routines, and relations vis-à-vis multiple messages.

— Incentives foster motivation among all participants in interventions.

— The teaching of skills is crucial to support behavior change.

— Leadership support is essential for program success.

— Community participation builds local awareness and ownership. Integrating support from different stakeholders sets apart social marketing from commercial advertising as it aims to be integrated with community initiatives.

— Feedback makes it possible to improve and refine programs.

Health promotion and health education: The trajectory of health promotion in development communication resembles the move of social marketing and diffusion of innovation, from originally gaining influence in the United States to being introduced in interventions in developing countries. The same approaches that were used to battle chronic diseases, high-fat diets, and smoking in the United States in the 1970s and 1980s, were adopted in development interventions such as child survival and other programs that aimed to remedy health problems in the Third World. As it crystallized in the Lalonde report in Canada in 1974 and the U.S. Surgeon General's 1979 Healthy People report, health promotion was dominated by the view that individual behavior was largely responsible for health problems and, consequently, interventions should focus on changing behavior. It approached health in terms of disease problems (rather than health generally), namely, the existence of lifestyle behaviors (smoking, heavy drinking, poor diet) that had damaging consequences for individual, and by extension, social health.

The prevalent view was that changes in personal behaviors were needed to have a healthier population. Although the idea that institutional changes were also necessary to achieve that goal made strides, health promotion remained focused on personal change at the expense of community actions and responsibility. A substantial number of studies were offered as conclusive evidence that personal choices determined changes in health behavior, and were positively related with new developments that indicated the decrease of unhealthy practices. This highly individualistic perspective was initially criticized in the context of developed countries for "blaming the victim" and ignoring social conditions that facilitated and encouraged unhealthy behaviors. It gave a free ride to larger social and political processes that were responsible for disease and essentially depoliticized the question of health behavior. To its critics, individual-centered health promotion ignores the surrounding social context (poverty, racism) in which individual health behaviors take place as well as the fact that certain unhealthy behaviors are more likely to be found among certain groups. They pointed out that the overall context needed to be considered both as responsible and as the possible target of change.

Recent understandings of health promotion such as the one promoted by the World Health Organization have moved away from individualistic views by stressing the idea that individual and social actions need to be integrated. The goal of health promotion is to provide and maintain conditions that make it possible for people to make healthy choices. Health education is an important component of health promotion. It refers to learning experiences to facilitate individual adoption of healthy behaviors.

The evolution of health education somewhat mirrored the evolution of the field of development communication. Health education was initially dominated by conventional educational approaches that, like modernization/diffusion models, were influenced by individual behaviorist models that emphasized knowledge transmission and acquisition as well as changes in knowledge, attitudes and beliefs. Later, theories and strategies that stressed the importance of social and environmental changes gained relevance. This meant that both health education and health promotion became more broadly understood.

Health education includes different kinds of interventions such as conventional education, social marketing, health communication, and empowerment actions. Consequently, a vast range of activities such as peer education, training of health workers, community mobilization, and social marketing are considered examples of health education interventions.

Health promotion became no longer understood as limited to educational efforts and individual changes. It also includes the promotion of public policies that are responsible for shaping a healthy environment. The goal of health promotion is to facilitate the environmental conditions to support healthy behaviors. Individual knowledge, as conceived in traditional approaches, is insufficient if groups lack basic systems that facilitate the adoption of healthy practices. The mobilization of a diversity of social forces including families and communities is necessary to shape a healthy environment.

The emphasis on social mobilization to improve general conditions does not mean that behavior change models are absent in health promotion but, rather, that they need to be integrated among other strategies. Still, the behavior change model has incorporated the idea that interventions need to be sensitive to the education and the choices of receivers, understanding the interests at stake, using social marketing technique to know individuals better, and the role of the community in interventions.

Entertainment education: Entertainment-education is another strategy that shares behavior-change premises with the forementioned theories and strategies. Entertainment-education is a communication strategy to disseminate information through the media. As applied in development communication, it was originally developed in Mexico in the mid-1970s and has been used in 75 countries, including India, Nigeria, the Philippines, Turkey, Gambia, and Pakistan. Paradigmatic examples of this approach have been soap operas in Latin America (telenovelas) and in India that were intended to provide information about family planning, sexual behavior, and health issues. Literacy and agricultural development have also been central themes of several entertainment education efforts.

Entertainment-education is not a theory but a strategy to maximize the reach and effectiveness of health messages through the combination of entertainment and education. The fact that its premises are derived from socio-psychology and human communication theories place entertainment-education in the modernization/diffusion theory trunk. It subscribes to the Shannon-Weaver model of communication of senderchannel-message-receiver. Like diffusion theory, it is concerned with behavior change through the dissemination of information. It is based on Stanford Professor Albert Bandura's social learning theory, a framework currently dominant in health promotion.

Entertainment-education is premised on the idea that individuals learn behavior by observing role models, particularly in the mass media. Imitation and influence are the expected outcomes of interventions. Entertainment-education telenovelas were based on Bandura's model of cognitive sub-processes: attention, retention, production and motivational processes that help understand why individuals imitate socially desirable behavior. This process depends on the existence of role models in the messages: good models, bad models, and those who transition from bad to good. Besides social learning, entertain-education strategies are based on the idea that expected changes result from self-efficacy, the belief of individuals that they can complete specific tasks.

Entertainment-education refers to "the process of purposely designing and implementing a media message to both entertain and educate, in order to increase audience knowledge about an educational issue, create favorable attitudes, and change overt behavior". Like social marketing and health promotion, it is concerned with social change at individual and community levels. Its focus is on how entertainment media such as soap operas, songs, cartoons, comics and theater can be used to transmit information that can result in pro-social behavior. Certainly, the use of entertainment for social purposes is not new as they have been used for centuries. What is novel is the systematic research and implementation of educational, pro-social messages in entertainment media in the developed world.

One of the starting points of entertainment-education is that populations around the world are widely exposed to entertainment media content. The heavy consumption of media messages suggests that the media have an unmatched capacity to tell people how to dress, talk and think. The problem is, as numerous studies document, that entertainment messages are rarely positive. In the attempt to maximize audiences by appealing to the lowest common denominator, the media are filled with anti-social messages such as violence, racism, stereotyping, and sexual promiscuity. However, the pervasiveness of the media provides numerous opportunities to communicate messages that can help people in solving a myriad of problems that they confront.

Another central premise is that education does not necessarily need to be dull but it can incorporate entertainment formats to generate pro-social attitudes and behavior. This could solve the problem that audiences find social messages uninteresting and boring, and prefer to consume entertainment media. What characterizes the latter is the intention of the messages (to divert rather than to educate) and to capture audiences' interest. These characteristics should not be dismissed as superficial and mindless but need to be closely examined to analyze the potential of entertainment to educate the public in an engaging manner. Moreover, because they are entertaining and widely popular, entertainment-education messages can also be profitable for television networks and other commercial ventures.

Simplemente María, a 1969 Peruvian telenovela, has been often mentioned as having pioneered entertainment-education even though it was not intended to have pro-social effects. The protagonist was a maid who attended night sewing classes. The program has been credited with having turned sewing into a craze among poor, migrant women as well as increasing the purchase of sewing machines and contributing to higher enrollment numbers in literacy classes. This example and subsequent ones were deemed to be important in two regards. The programs contribute to self-efficacy (an individual's belief that he or she is able to take action and control specific outcomes) and social learning (individuals not only learn through their own experiences but also by observing and imitating the behavior of other individuals as role models).

Besides television entertainment, entertainment-education interventions were also implemented in music and music videos promoting sexual control, and radio soap operas that promoted women's issues, AIDS and sex education, and family planning. In the mid-1980s, a campaign was implemented to promote sexual restraint among Mexican teenagers. It consisted of songs and music videos featuring a male and female singer as well as public service announcements. Evaluation analysis concluded that the campaign had a number of positive consequences: teenagers felt freer to talk about sex, became more sensitized about the relevance of sex, messages reinforced teenagers who already practiced abstinence, and demand for family planning services modestly increased.

Comparable findings were documented in a similar intervention in the Philippines. The campaign also featured songs, video, live presentations of the performers, and PSAs. It resulted in positive changes in knowledge, attitude and behavior. Other less effective campaigns suggested that appeals that may work in some cultural contexts could fail in others. Performers need to be credible, that is, audiences need to believe that they truly represent the values promoted.

Some studies have concluded that entertainment-education strategies are successful in attracting large audiences, triggering interpersonal communication about issues and lessons from interventions, and in engaging and motivating individuals to change behavior and support changes among their peers. Rogers et al. concluded that a soap-opera radio broadcast in Tanzania played an important role in fertility changes. The broadcast increased listeners' sense of self-efficacy, ideal age at marriage of women, approval contraceptive use, interspousal communication about family planning, and current practice of family planning.

Similarly, Piotrow et al. report that the "Male Motivation Project" in Zimbabwe, which involved a radio drama intended to influence men's decisions in opting for different reproductive choices, resulted in changes in beliefs and attitudes. Also, Valente et al found that individuals who listened to a radio drama in the Gambia have better knowledge, attitudes and practices than the control group. The study also concluded that substantial changes in use of contraceptive methods existed after the broadcast.

Both studies concluded that audiences incorporate language presented in the programming, talk to others, and introduce behavior changes. A hierarchy of effects was observed in interventions in Mexico, Nigeria and the Philippines. In decreasing order, campaigns contributed to audience recall, comprehension, agreement, and talking with others about the messages promoted in the campaigns. In contrast, other studies have found little evidence that entertainment education strategies have resulted in such effects.

Yoder and coauthors have argued that the changes in behavior reported in the Zimbabwe and Gambia studies were not statistically significant. An analysis of the impact of a radio drama in Zambia suggested that improvement in knowledge and awareness about AIDS could not be directly attributed to the intervention. Significant changes in condom use were not associated with exposure to the radio drama as there was a substantial amount of information and public debate about HIV/AIDS during the time the drama was broadcast. Exposure to discrete radio programs per se did not account for changes between target and control groups. Moreover, a return to previous behavior after the broadcast suggested the lack of evidence of long-term impact and attributed the findings to the timing when the data were collected.

Exposure to entertainment-education messages was positively associated with use of modern contraceptive methods but the data did not allow a direct causal inference. It was not clear whether the campaign had influenced knowledge and practices. Studies did not reject the possible counter-explanation that people more predisposed to family planning were more likely to be exposed and recall media content.

Rather than discounting the possibility of any media effects, Yoder and associates concluded that it is problematic to reach comprehensive conclusions about the effectiveness of entertainment education. In contrast to more optimistic evaluations that suggest that the task ahead is to measure what works better, they recommended a more cautionary approach. Entertainment-education projects are effective in stimulating people predisposed to change behavior to engage in a new behavior (e.g. use contraceptive methods). They provide the push for those already inclined to act to behave differently. Media interventions catalyze latent demand into contraceptive use among ready-to-act populations.

Beginning in the late 1960s, the field of development communication split in two broad approaches: one that revised but largely continued the premises and goals of modernization and diffusion theories, and another that has championed a participatory view of communication in contrast to information- and behavior-centered theories. Both approaches have dominated the field. Although in recent years there have been attempts to incorporate insights from both traditions, no comprehensive view has evolved.

Dependency Theory

One of the most powerful critiques of modernization/ diffusion theories came from the dependency paradigm. Originally developed in Latin America, dependency analysis was informed by Marxist and critical theories according to which the problems of the Third World reflected the general dynamics of capitalist development. Development problems responded to the unequal distribution of resources created by the global expansion of Western capitalism.

Dependency theorists argued that the problems of underdevelopment were not internal to Third World countries but were determined by external factors and the way former colonies were integrated into the world economy. It forcefully stated that the problems of the underdeveloped world were political rather than the result of the lack of information. What kept Third World countries underdeveloped were social and economic factors, namely the dominated position that those countries had in the global order. Underdevelopment, they argued, was the flip side and the consequence of the development of the Western world. The latter concentrated economic power and political decisions that maintained underdevelopment and dependency. Third world countries were politically and culturally dependent on the West, particularly on the United States.

Asides from external problems, internal structures were also responsible for the problems of underdevelopment. Dependency positions charged development programs for failing to address structures of inequality and targeting individual rather than social factors. Unequal land distribution, lack of credit for peasants, and poor health care services strongly limited the possibilities for an overall improvement in social conditions. Interventions were doomed when basic conditions that could make it possible for people to adopt new attitudes and behaviors were missing.

Innovations promoted by development programs were adopted by individuals from higher socioeconomic strata living in cities rather than by rural and poor populations. In singling out the mass media as having a central role in introducing innovations, modernization theories ignored the issue of media ownership and control. Urban and powerful interests controlled the media that was supposed to promote development.

The media were not interested in championing social goals or helping underprivileged populations but in transmitting entertainment and trivial information. The relation between media structure and content was virtually ignored in modernization theories. Only a small percentage of programming was devoted to development issues and in regions such as Latin America, the media were commercially run and their the central goal was profit-making not social change.

For dependency theorists, modernization theories was driven by behaviorist, positivist and empiricist approaches in the mold of the "scientific model" that prevailed in U.S.

universities and research centers. These particular biases accounted for why structural factors were ignored and for why interventions were focused on behavior changes at the individual level rather than on social causes of poverty and marginalization.

Modernization theories as applied in the Third World featured, to quote Bolivian communication researcher Luis Ramiro Beltrán, "alien premises, objects and methods." The solution to underdevelopment problems was essentially political, rather than merely informational. What was required was social change in order to transform the general distribution of power and resources. Information and media policies were necessary to deal with communication problems.

Solutions to underdevelopment required major changes in media structures that were dominated by commercial principles and foreign interests. Policies needed to promote national and public goals that could put the media in the service of the people rather than as pipelines for capitalist ideologies. Such positions were expressed in a number of international fora, particularly during the UNESCO-sponsored debates about the New World Information and Communication Order in the 1970s and 1980s. Representatives from Third Wolrd countries proposed "national communication policies" that emphasized the need for governments to control media structures and oppose domestic and foreign elites and business interests.

Participatory Theories and Approaches

Participatory theories also criticized the modernization paradigm on the grounds that it promoted a top-down, ethnocentric and paternalistic view of development. They argued that the diffusion model proposed a conception of development associated with a Western vision of progress. Development communication was informed by a theory that "became a science of producing effective messages".

After decades of interventions, the failure to address poverty and other structural problems in the Third World needed to be explained on the faulty theoretical premises of the programs. Any intervention that was focused on improving messages to better reach individuals or only change behavior was, by definition, unable to implement social change.

Development theories also criticized traditional approaches for having been designed and executed in the capital cities by local elites with guidance and direction from foreign specialists. Local people were not involved in preparing and instrumenting development interventions. Interventions basically conceived of local residents as passive receivers of decisions made outside of their communities, and in many cases, instrumented illconceived plans to achieve development. Governments decided what was best for agricultural populations, for example, without giving them a sense of ownership in the systems that were introduced.

The top-down approach of persuasion models implicitly assumed that the knowledge of governments and agencies was correct, and that indigenous populations either did not know or had incorrect beliefs. Because programs came from outside villages, communities felt that innovations did not belong to them but to the government and thus expected the latter to fix things went they went wrong. The sense of disempowerment was also rooted in the fact that "targeted" populations did not have the choice to reject recommendations or introduce modifications to interventions.

For participatory theorists and practitioners, development communication required sensitivity to cultural diversity and specific context that were ignored by modernization theories. The lack of such sensitivity accounted for the problems and failures of many projects. Experts learnt that development was not restricted to just building roads, piping water, and distributing electricity. Nor was it limited to efforts to increase farm yields nor switching farmers over to cash crops. Many of the agricultural projects failed because farmers were reluctant to abandon their traditional ways for foreign and unknown methods.

As McKee writes, "they were also nervous about planting exotic crops that they could not eat but had to sell for money with which to buy food from the market." Modernization projects undermined the importance of local knowledge and the consequences of the interaction between local cultures and foreign ideas. When piped water arrived, it was frequently used for washing rather than drinking and cooking because the people disliked its flavor. Persuading people of the benefits of healthy practices on the basis of scientific reasons was a tough sell. People were asked to change time-old practices on the basis of a foreign form of knowledge that dismissed their local traditions in the name of "true" knowledge.

The lack of local participation was viewed as responsible for the failure of different programs. In the case of agricultural programs, it was concluded that the issue at stake was not the transmission of information to increase output but rather the low prices of agricultural goods in the market or the absence of a more equal distribution of land ownership. In explaining the failures of family planning programs, it was suggested that mothers were disinclined to follow instructions because fathers believed that having more children meant having more hands to work in the fields and carry out other tasks.

Participatory theories considered necessary a redefinition of development communication. One set of definitions stated that it meant the systematic utilization of communication channels and techniques to increase people's participation in development and to inform, motivate, and train rural populations mainly at the grassroots. For others, development communication needed to be human- rather than mediacentered. This implied the abandonment of the persuasion bias that development communication had inherited from propaganda theories, and the adoption of a different understanding of communication.

Communication means a process of creating and stimulating understanding as the basis for development rather than information transmission. Communication is the articulation of social relations among people. People should not be forced to adopt new practices no matter how beneficial they seem in the eyes of agencies and governments. Instead, people needed to be encouraged to participate rather than adopt new practices based on information.

This understanding of communication was central to the ideas developed by Brazilian educator Paulo Freire, whose writings and experiences became an influential strand in participatory communication. Freire's work in northeastern Brazil in the 1960s and early 1970s challenged dominant conceptions of development communication, particularly as applied to literacy training. He argued that development programs had failed to educate small farmers because they were interested in persuading them about the benefits of adopting certain innovations.

Development programs tried to domesticate foreign concepts, to feed information, to force local populations to accept Western ideas and practices without asking how such practices fit existing cultures. The underlying premise of such programs was an authoritarian conception of communication that stood against the essence of communication understood as community interaction and education.

Freire offered the concept of liberating education that conceived communication as dialogue and participation. The goal of communication should be conscientization, which Freire defined as free dialogue that prioritized cultural identity, trust and commitment. His approach has been called "dialogical pedagogy" which defined equity in distribution and active grassroots participation as central principles. Communication should provide a sense of ownership to participants through sharing and reconstructing experiences.

Education is not transmission of information from those "who have it" to those "who lack it," from the powerful to the powerless, but the creative discovery of the world. Freire's ideas ran against fundamental principles in the diffusion model, namely the sender-focus and behavioral bias that it inherited from persuasion models in the United States. He diagnosed the problems in the Third World as problems of communication, not information as persuasion theories proposed. Solutions, then, needed to have an understanding of communication that was not limited to the application of Western ideas. Freire also challenged the value judgment in early development theories that viewed agricultural and health practices in the Third World as backwards and obstacles to modernization.

Freire's model and participatory models in general proposed a human-centered approach that valued the importance of interpersonal channels of communication in decisionmaking processes at the community level. Studies in a variety of Third World rural settings found that marginal and illiterate groups preferred to communicate face-to-face rather than through mass media or other one-way sources of communication. The recommendation was that development workers should rely more on interpersonal methods of communication rather than national media and technologies, and that they should act as facilitators of dialogue.

Because media and technologies were perceived as foreign to local communities, they should be used to supplement instead of dominate interpersonal methods. The notion of "group media" drew from Freire to call the media that are means for small groups to develop a critical attitude towards the reality of self, the group, community and society through participation in group interaction. Group media has helped marginal groups to speak to one another, to articulate their thoughts and feelings in the process of community organizing.

Community-based forms of communication such as songs, theater, radio, video, and other activities that required group intervention needed to be promoted. More than mechanisms to disseminate information, they could provide opportunities to identify common problems and solution, to reflect upon community issues, and mobilize resources. Community members, rather than "professionals", should be in charge of the decision and production processes. This is precisely what "small" media offer: an opportunity for media access in countries where the mass media are usually controlled by governments and urban elites.

The value of participatory media is not in being instruments of transmission but of communication, that is, for exchanging views and involving members. Community media dealt with various subjects: literacy, health, safety, agricultural productivity, land ownership, gender, and religion. There have been a number of paradigmatic examples. In Latin America, miners' and peasants' radio in Bolivia, grassroots video in peasant and indigenous movements in Brazil, tape recorders in Guatemala, small-scale multimedia in Peru and other cases of low-powered media based in unions and churches were offered as concrete examples of participatory communication development. Canada's "Fogo process" was another experience informed by similar principles in which populations living in remote areas actively produced videos to discuss community issues of people living in remote areas and to communicate with outsiders about their concerns and expectations. In Africa, popular theater has been successfully used to increase women's participation and ability to deal with primary care problems. Through songs and storytelling, women were able to raise awareness and attention to issues and address problems, something that had not been achieved through "modern" media such as television and newspapers.

Community participation through popular theater motivated rural communities to become involved in health care. Participation was credited for the reduction of preventable diseases such as cholera and severe diarrhea after communities constructed infrastructure that helped to improve sanitary conditions situation. In stressing the relevance of "other" media and forms of communication, participatory theories lifted development communication out of the "large media" and "stimulusresponse" straitjacket and opened new ways of understanding interventions. They expanded the concept of participation that in modernization theories was limited to voting in party and electoral politics and championed a view of democracy that implied different forms of participation at different levels.

They also removed professionals and practitioners from having a central role as transmitters of information who would enlighten populations in development projects. People, not change agents, were central to community participation. It downplayed the role of expert and external knowledge while stressing the centrality of indigenous knowledge and aspirations in development. Communication was a horizontal process, diametrically different from the vertical model that placed knowledge in the domain of modern experts.

Participatory communication identified encouraging participation, stimulating critical thinking, and stressing process, rather than specific outcomes associated with modernization and progress, as the main tasks of development communication. Participation needed to be present in all stages of development projects. Communities should be encouraged to participate in decision-making, implementation, and evaluation of projects. This would give a sense of involvement in their lives and communities, and provide them with a sense of ownership and skills that they can use beyond the timetable of development projects.

Community empowerment has become became one of the main contributions of participatory theories to development communication. Empowerment is possible only if community members critically reflect on their experiences and understand the reasons for failure and success of interventions. Certainly, participatory communication has not lacked critics. Even though vindicating some tenets of participatory theories, other positions argued that they were elaborated at a theoretical level and did not provide specific guidelines for interventions.

One problem in participatory models was that it was not clear that communities needed to be involved for certain results to be achieved. In some cases such as epidemics and other public health crises, quick and top-down solutions could achieve positive results. Participation communication ignores that expediency may also positively contribute to development. Belaboring through grassroots decision-making process is slower than centralized decisions, and thus not advisable in cases that require prompt resolutions. Participation might be a good long-term strategy but has shortcomings when applied to short-term and urgent issues.

Another problem was that participation in all stages does not have similar relevance. It was not clear what participation entailed. If decisions were made outside of the community and the latter was assigned the role of implementing and evaluating results, some positions argued, participation was limited to instances that depended on decisions previously made. It was not true participation and, therefore, maintained power inequalities.

Another problem was that the focus on interpersonal relations underplayed the potential of the mass media in promoting development as participation and process. Little attention was paid to the uses of mass media in participatory settings, an issue that is particularly relevant considering that populations, even in remote areas, are constantly exposed to commercial media messages that stand in opposition to the goals set by programs. This lack was particularly evident in Freire's theory of dialogical communication that is based on group interactions and underplays the role of the mass media.

Participatory approaches usually avoided the issue that people who lived in nondemocratic societies might be were wary to participate out of fear of retaliation. Moreover, people can be manipulated into participating. This would violate local autonomy and the possibility that members might not be interested in taking an active role.

Critics argued that participatory communication, like social marketing, could also be seen as foreign, pushing for certain goals and actions that have not resulted from inside communities. Participatory communication did not offer the chance not to participate, and implicitly coerced people to adopt a certain attitude.

Social marketers charged that participatory approaches were too idealistic, falling short from offering specific practical guidelines, and offering recommendations with limited impact. These shortcoming are particularly pronounced when funds for development communication are short and funding agencies are interested in obtaining cost-effective results not just at the local but also the national level.

Other critics, particularly in Asia, thought that participatory models were premised on Western-styled ideas of democracy and participation that do not fit political cultures elsewhere. Individualism rather than community and conflict rather than consensus lie at the heart of participatory models developed in the West. Participation can also promote division, confusion, and disruption that do little to solve problems. It may privilege powerful and active members of the community at the expense of the community as a whole. Education and decision-making skills, rather than participation for its own sake, should be promoted.

To these criticisms, advocates of participatory models admitted that divisions and conflicts might result but, they argued, the answer should be teaching negotiation and mediation skills rather than opting for interventions that disempower people in the name of consensus-building. Although advocates of participatory theories viewed their critics as favoring government centralization and leaving power inequalities intact, they admitted that some original premises needed to be revised.

Participatory approaches needed to:

— Be sensitive to the potential convenience of short-term and rapid solutions. Recognize that recommendations for participation could also be seen as foreign and manipulative by local communities (just like modernization theories). Translate participatory ideas into actual programs.

— Be aware that the communities may be uninterested in spending time in democratic processes of decision-making and, instead, might prefer to invest their time on other activities.

— Recognize that communities are not necessarily harmonious and that participation may actually deepen divisions. Servaes admits that "participation does not always entail cooperation nor consensus. It can often mean conflict and usually poses a threat to existent structures...Rigid and general strategies for participation are neither possible nor desirable."

— To prevent some of these problems, it was suggested that it was preferable that projects be carried out in communities where agencies already had linkages.

Previous knowledge of problems and characteristics of a given community was fundamental to identify activities and define projects. Existing linkages could also provide agents that were familiar with (or even were from) the community who could assist in creating organizations and networks to stimulate participation. No previously determined set of activities was advisable if the interests and dynamics of communities were not known. Workers would also provide important feedback information about the progress of projects through regular, face-to-face contact with participants. These practices function as a sort of transmission belt for making sure that community issues are addressed and that members have a voice in deciding future courses. The peril is to focus solely on professional technicians and leaders without consideration of involving the community at large.

Against criticisms that participatory communication leads to the existence of a myriad, disconnected projects carried out by multiple NGOs, coordination plans were deemed necessary. Providing a sense of orientation and organization was required to prevent that development efforts become too fragmented and thus weaker. Because NGOs are closer to communities than governments and funding agencies, they have the capacity to respond relatively quickly to demands and developments. But without a more encompassing vision, projects may only obtain, at best, localized results that fail to have a larger impact.

It was also recommended that relying on grassroots media was not sufficient. Populations needed media education to develop skills to be critical of commercial media and to develop alternatives that would help them gain a sense of empowerment and counter other messages. Yet, it was undeniable that local media provided a sense of ownership and participation that was key to sustainable development and could not be replaced by any other strategy.

Responding to critics who were impatient with obtaining "results," participatory approaches suggested that development communication requires a long-term perspective that is usually missing among funding agencies and governments interested in getting quick results and knowing whether efforts pay off. Participatory theorists turned the criticisms about "timing" and "impact" onto their critics, arguing that the so-called problems of participatory approaches in "showing results" did not originate in the model but in how organizations approach development communication.

Shortterm projects that are prone to be terminated according to different considerations make it difficult to promote participation and examine the results of interventions in the long run. The interests of funders and politicians, who were urged to prove effectiveness of investments, ran against the timing of participatory development communication projects. For the latter to be possible, NGOs, funding agencies and other actors involved needed to be sensitive to the fact that grassroots projects cannot be expected to "produce results" in the manner of top-down interventions. Neither community development nor empowerment fit the timetables of traditional programs.

Media Advocacy Approach

Media advocacy is another approach that questions central premises of the traditional paradigm. Media advocacy is the strategic use of mass media to advance social or public policy initiatives. Its goals are to stimulate debate and promote responsible portrayals and coverage of health issues. Advocacy requires the mobilization of resources and groups in support of certain issues and policies to change public opinion and decisions. It consists of the organization of information for dissemination through various interpersonal and media channels towards gaining political and social acceptance of certain issues.

Like education-entertainment strategies, media advocacy rejects the idea that the media can be a source of only anti-social messages, and instead, proposes to include socially relevant themes in entertainment. Both share the perspective that because the media are the main source of information about health issues, interventions need to focus on the media. Both also believe in the capacity of the media to transmit information that can result in changes.

Unlike education-entertainment, which has been mostly concerned with directly influencing audiences, media advocacy centers on shaping the public debate about public health. It is not information-centered but aims to incorporate social themes in entertainment content in order to influence public agendas. It takes a political and social approach that differs from the social-psychological premises and diagnoses found in education-entertainment.

And, in contrast to education-entertainment, it is less convinced about the power of the media to be extremely effective in changing attitudes and behavior.

Because it locates problems in political and social conditions, social advocacy promotes social, rather than individual and behavioral, changes to health issues. It approaches health not as a personal issue but as a matter of social justice. It is explicitly set against the individualistic assumptions of mainstream approaches found in the dominant paradigm of development communication that fault individuals for unhealthy and antisocial behaviors and propose individual solutions based on the idea that health is primarily a question of individual responsibility. Instead, it advocates changes in the social environment that legitimize certain behaviors. For example, it sees tobacco and alcohol companies rather than individual smokers and drinkers as responsible for unhealthy behavior. Therefore, those companies should be the targets of advocacy and communication activities. Actions should target, for example, access to unhealthy products by involving communities in implementing policy changes.

Here the contrast with behavior-centered health approaches is clear as media advocacy proposes that social conditions should be the target of interventions. Such interventions entail fundamentally a political process of changing conditions and redressing social inequalities rather persuading individuals about the benefits of certain lifestyles and behavior change. Health is a matter of social justice and partnering with interested parties rather than providing information to change individual behavior.

These premises set media advocacy apart from social marketing. Media advocacy criticizes social marketing for having an individualistic, behaviorist approach to health and social problems that narrows interventions to public information campaigns. Media advocacy espouses a community-level model of intervention in health issues. Development, defined to be the well being of communities, can be achieved through promoting structures and policies that support healthy lifestyles. Community organization is the process by which community groups are helped to identify common problems or goals, mobilize resources, and develop and implement strategies for reaching their goals.

According to media advocacy theory, campaigns are not the panacea not only because their effectiveness is questionable but also because they ignore the social causes of unhealthy behavior. Public service announcements have shown limited success in stimulating change and fail to address the social and economic environment that ultimately determines health risk factors.

Social marketing does not face head-on the fundamental structures that sustain unhealthy behavior. Social advocacy does not minimize the importance of individual changes but, instead, it strongly argues that the latter require changes in social conditions. Because external conditions are responsible for health, the strategy should target those conditions instead of centering on lifestyle behaviors. Promoting individual health habits in developing countries without, for example, advocating for clean water supplies underplays the factors responsible for disease.

Media advocacy adopts a participatory approach that emphasizes the need of communities to gain control and power to transform their environments. It assigns the media a pivotal role in raising issues that need to be discussed and putting pressure on decision-makers. However, advocacy is not solely concerned with media actions. Because it concludes that health problems are fundamentally rooted in power inequalities, it promotes a dual strategy to build power that includes the formation of coalitions and grassroots actions coupled with media actions and lobbying.

Media advocacy theory assumes that the media largely shape public debate and, consequently, political and social interventions. To be politically effective, then, influencing news agendas is mandatory. AIDS and tobacco control coalitions and groups in the United States have been successful in their use of the mass media that has resulted in support, funding and the implementation of public policies.

Media-savviness is necessary to get widespread coverage of certain health issues and to shape how stories are presented. Here again social advocacy differs from social marketing. Social advocacy is not about putting in action centralized actions to relay information to consumers but, rather, providing skills to communities so they can influence media coverage. It approaches the media not in terms of "health messages" but as agenda-setters of policy initiatives. Placing messages is not only insufficient to correct problems but it is also the wrong strategy: the target of media interventions should be news divisions rather than the advertising departments of media organizations.

Moreover, the media might be willing to feature public service announcements for a variety of reasons to further its own goals. Lobbying the media to feature PSAs does not necessarily result in an examination of structural conditions responsible for health problems, however.

Media interest in participating in health promotion activities by donating free airtime fall short from moving away from the individualistic view that dominates behavior change models. Such contributions by media organizations do not deal with external factors, unequal access and structures, and the political environment that is ultimately responsible for public health problems. This is why public health needs to incorporate a broader view that conceives actions in terms of community participation and mobilization to transform public opinion and change health policies.

In summary, advocacy consists of a large number of information activities, such as lobbying with decision makers through personal contacts and direct mail; holding seminars, rallies and newsmaking events; ensuring regular newspaper, magazine, television and radio coverage and obtaining endorsements from known people. The goal of advocacy is to make the innovation a political or national priority that cannot be swept aside with a change in government. In the context of development programs, media advocacy may be carried out by key people in international agencies, as well as special ambassadors, but is gradually taken over by people in national and local leadership positions and the print and electronic media.

Social Mobilization

Social mobilization is a term used by the United Nations International Children's Emergency Fund (UNICEF) to describe a comprehensive planning approach that emphasizes political coalition building and community action. It is the process of bringing together all feasible and practical inter-sectoral social allies to raise people's awareness of and demand for a particular development program, to assist in the delivery of resources and services and to strengthen community participation for sustainability and self-reliance. A successful mobilization must be built on the basis of mutual benefits of partners and a decentralized structure. The more interested the partners are, the more likely that a project of social mobilization can be sustained over time. This approach does not require that partners abandon their own interests and perceptions on a given issue but are willing to coalesce around a certain problem. One of the basic requisites is that groups carefully consider the best-suited groups to partner for a specific program.

A child survival and development program in Ghana, for example, started with an analysis to identify individuals and organizations with the potential to serve as partners in a social mobilization project. The study included three sub-studies: interviews with members of governmental institutions, trade unions, revolutionary organizations, and traditional leaders among others; media content analysis that suggested the need for collective efforts between journalists and health workers; and the assessment of health information sources among parents. It concluded that partners included religious organizations, women's groups, and school teachers.

Mobilization is a process through which community members become aware of a problem, identify the problem as a high priority for community action, and decide steps to take action. It starts with problem assessment and analysis at the community level and moves to action on chosen courses, involving many strategic allies at all levels in a wide range of support activities. Central to social mobilization interventions is empowerment or the process through which individuals or communities take direct contorl over their lives and environment.

Social mobilization suggests that wide community participation is necessary for members to gain ownership so innovations would not be seen as externally imposed. Community mobilization is one of the main resources in implementing behavior change. Social mobilization differs from traditional social marketing approaches that are largely based on appeals to individuals. When there is no individual interest in adopting innovations and, particularly in the context of developing countries, reaching people only through social marketing techniques is not effective, interpersonal channels stimulated by social mobilization allow the wide diffusion of concepts and innovations and increasing demand.

Social mobilization is closely interlinked with media advocacy. To McKee, social mobilization "is the glue that binds advocacy activities to more planned and researched program communication activities." It strengthens advocacy efforts and relates them to social marketing activities. It makes it possible to add efforts from different groups to reach all levels of society by engaging in different activities: service delivery, mobilizing resources providing new channels for communication; providing training and logistical support for field workers, and managing field workers.

Examples of social mobilization interventions include World Bank nutrition and family planning projects in Bangladesh that also used a social mobilization approach by assigned non-governmental organizations (NGOs) the role of mobilizing communities. It defined community mobilization as "the process of involving and motivating interested stakeholders (general public, health workers, policy-makers, etc.) to organize and take action for a common purpose.

Mobilization of communities should focus on building confidence, trust and respect, increasing knowledge base, and enabling community members to participate, and become more proactive with regard to their own health behavior." The implementation required to identify and utilize village communication networks, train field workers, locate and mobilize opinion leaders, activate link persons, establish rotating peer group discussions, provide information and supplies at meetings.

Theoretical Convergence

Since the 1950s, the meaning of development communication has changed. Changes should not be surprising considering that "development," a concept that together with "modernization" and "Third World" emerged and dominated academic and policy debates in the 1950s, has lost much of its past luster. New concepts have been coined and gained popularity but have not displaced the broad notion of development communication.

Despite its multiple meanings, development communication remains a sort of umbrella term to designate research and interventions concerned with improving conditions among people struggling with economic, social political problems in the non-Western world. Like "development," "communication" has also undergone important transformations in the past five decades that reflected the ebbs and flows of intellectual and political debates as well as the changing fortunes of theoretical approaches.

The absence of a widespread consensus in defining "development" and "communication" reflect the larger absence of a common vocabulary in the field. This conceptual ambiguity and confusion should not be surprising considering that different disciplines and theories have converged in the field of development communication. There has been a confluence of overlapping traditions from a variety of disciplines that imported vocabularies that had little in common.

The presence of different terminologies does not necessarily reflect opposite understandings but, mainly, the existence of different trunks in the family tree. In a fragmented field, diverse programs and strategies are rooted in a myriad of intellectual fields that were rarely in fluid contact. Despite the diversity of origins, however, it is remarkable that there has been a tendency towards having a more comprehensive understanding of "development communication."

The historic gap between approaches has not been bridged but, certainly, there have been visible efforts to integrate dissimilar models and strategies. Consider Jan Servaes' definition of development as a multidimensional process that involves change in social structures, attitudes, institution, economic growth, reduction of inequality, and the eradication of poverty. For him, development is a "whole change for a better life." This notion comes close to the idea of "another development" that emphasizes the satisfaction of needs, endogenous self-reliance, and life in harmony with the environment.

We would be hard-pressed to find approaches and interventions that essentially disagree with such encompassing idea of development. Similarly, different approaches have gradually adopted an understanding of communication that is not reduced to the idea of information transmission, but includes the idea of process and exchange. Certainly, the persuasion model of communication maintains a towering presence in the field. Socio-psychological models of behavior and perspectives grounded in stimulus-response communication theories continue to dominate, arguably because some premises of the "dominant paradigm" remain widely accepted. The model of top-down, sender-receiver communication has been revised, however.

The idea of "communication as process" has gained centrality in approaches informed by both behavior change and participatory models. Moemeka's words illustrate a widespread sentiment in the field: "Communication should be seen both an independent and dependent variable. It can and does affect situations, attitudes, and behavior, and its content, context, direction, and flow are also affected by prevailing circumstances.

More importantly, communication should be viewed as an integral part of development plans –a part whose major objective is to create systems, modes, and strategies that could provide opportunities for the people to have access to relevant channels, and to make use of these channels and the ensuing communication environment in improving the quality of their lives." This perspective is somewhat akin to "ritualistic" models of communication that prioritize the Latin roots of the word (as in "making common" through the exchange of meaning) that gained currency in the field of communication in the last decades.

Communication is understood as communities and individuals engaging in meaning-making. It is a horizontal, deinstitutionalized, multiple process in which senders and receivers have interchangeable roles, according to participatory theorist Jan Servaes. From a perspective rooted in behavior change models, Kincaid has similarly argued that all participants are senders and receivers. The difference lies in the fact that whereas approaches largely informed by the dominant paradigm continue to think of communication as a process that contributes to behavior change, participatory models are not primarily concerned with "behavior" but with transforming social conditions.

Another salient feature of recent studies in development communication is the increasing influence of theories and approaches that were originated or have been widely used in health communication. Health communication has received more attention than education or agriculture, issues that were central in early projects of development communication.

Certainly, issues such as literacy, agricultural productivity, violence are includes in many contemporary development plans. Behavior change, social marketing, and health promotion models have become increasingly influential in development communication, however. In a way, the growing centrality of health issues should not be surprising considering that family planning and nutrition, for example, have been dominant in the agenda of development communication since the 1960s.

Additionally, attention to HIV/AIDS since the 1980s further contributed to the ascendancy of health and healthrelated approaches in the field. On the one hand, this shift could be interpreted as a reflection of the priorities of funding agencies. Although further research is needed to support this finding, it seems that the presence of health issues and, consequently, the influence of health communication approaches express the agenda of development organizations. On the other hand, it can also be interpreted as a result of the emergence of a broader approach to health issues. The definition of health as "a state of well-being," widely cited in contemporary studies, allows a more comprehensive approach that includes issues such as illiteracy and poverty that were not integrated in early development communication projects.

Notwithstanding important persistent differences among theories and approaches, it is possible to identify several points of convergence that suggest possible directions in the field of international communication.

1. *The need of political will:* One point of convergence is that political will is necessary in order to bring about change. Development communication should not only be concerned with instrumenting specific outcomes as defined in the traditional paradigm, but also with the process by which communities become empowered to intervene and transform their environment. Community empowerment should be the intended outcome of interventions. This requires coming up with a set of indicators that measure the impact of interventions in terms of empowerment.

Empowerment lacks a single definition, however. It can refer to communities making decisions for themselves and acquiring knowledge (e.g. about health issues). Whereas for participatory/advocacy approaches empowerment involves changes in power distribution, behavior models use empowerment to represent ways for communities to change behavior, for example, discontinuing unhealthy practices. Advocates of social marketing suggest that marketing empower people by proving information and having constant feedback from consumers so they can be responsible for their well-being.

Because understandings of empowerment are different, expectations about interventions are different, too. If development requires redressing power inequalities, then, it conceivably takes longer time than interventions that aim to change knowledge, attitudes and practices. The pressures for relatively quick results and short-term impact of interventions are better suited for a particular understanding of empowerment (and thus development communication) which is more aligned with behavior change than participatory approaches. The slowness of policy and political changes required for more equal distribution of resources and decision-making, as advocated by participatory models, does not fit short-term expectations.

The problems of measuring results, however, are not unique to participatory strategies. Many observers have indicated that behavior change models have not satisfactorily answered the question of long-term effects. The lack of longitudinal studies that document changes over time makes it difficult to know the extent of the influence of interventions and environmental factors that could help reach solid conclusions about the long-term impact of communication strategies.

The debate over "results indicators" has not concluded and that no easy resolution seem in sight, reflects the persistence of disagreements over measuring development. Answers to questions such as "what are the right results?" are expected to be different given that, notwithstanding a growing consensus on the issues of community empowerment and horizontal communication as central to development communication, behavior change and participatory models still define the task of interventions in different terms. In other words, there continues to be a tension between approaches that are oriented to achieving results as measured in behavior change and those that prioritize the building of sustainable resources as the goal of programs.

2. *A "tool-kit" conception of strategies*: Another important point of convergence is the presence of a "tool-kit" conception of approaches within the behavior change tradition. Practitioners have realized that a multiplicity of strategies is needed to improve the quality of life of communities in developing countries. Rather than promoting specific theories and methodologies regardless of the problem at stake, there has been an emerging consensus that different techniques are appropriate in different contexts in order to deal with different problems and priorities.

Theories and approaches are part of a "tool kit" that is used according to different diagnoses. There is the belief that the tools that are used to support behavior change depend on the context in which the program is implemented, the priorities of funders, and the needs of the communities.For example, conventional educational interventions might be recommended in critical situations such as epidemics when large masses of people need to be reached in a short period of time. Such strategies, however, would be unlikely to solve structural, long-term health problems.

Social marketing could be useful to address certain issues (for example, increase rates of immunization) but is inadequate to address deeper problems of community participation that are ultimately responsible for permanent changes. It also can result in the problem that interventions conclude when public information campaigns are terminated.

One of the problems is that such interventions create a dependency on media programs; the alternative, then, is focusing on self-maintaining resources that are responsible for the sustainability of programs. Another problem is that even when social marketing strategies are successful at raising awareness, they do not last forever and, therefore, other support systems are necessary to maintain participation and communication.

Because of the limitations of social marketing, other strategies are needed to address the problem of empowering and politically involving different groups. Social mobilization, for example, offers a way to deal with certain issues such as education, sanitation, nutrition (including breastfeeding), family planning, respiratory problems, AIDS and diarrheal diseases. Still, the mobilization of a vast array of partners is necessary but this does not exclude the uses of media advocacy and social marketing to target specific problems.

A breastfeeding program in Brazil successfully integrated social mobilization and social marketing. As a result of the program, there was an increase in the median duration of breastfeeding and a reduction in infant mortality. Ministries and professional medical and nutrition groups participated in elaborating plans and stimulating actions at the national and state levels among their employees, members and associated institutions. At the community level, mothers' groups were formed and breastfeeding was promoted through extension workers, university students, the church and other voluntary groups.

Family planning programs in Egypt have been another example of successful integration of different approaches. After the intervention, the use of contraceptives doubled and the birthrate dropped from 39.8 to 27.5 percent in ten years. The achievements of the program have been attributed to fact that the Information, Education & Communication Center of the State Information Service used five tools, including the mass media, interpersonal communication, and entertainment-education.

The participation of the government, health organizations and religious groups was also considered to be responsible for the success of the program. The application of any prescriptive theory and methods might not work everywhere. Because of political and religious reasons, it is difficult to bring together a wide spectrum of forces to rally behind issues such as breastfeeding, family planning, and AIDS education in some countries. Under these circumstances, searching for a broad coalition is not recommended. In cases where governments strictly control the mass media or believe that they should be the only actors involved in public information campaigns, then, social marketing interventions confront many problems.

There has been a growing sensitivity to the problems of the universal application of strategies that were successful in specific contexts. In countries where political and cultural factors limit participation and maintain hierarchical relationships, participatory approaches might be difficult to implement as they require a long-term and highly political process of transformation. This does not mean that participation should be abandoned as a desirable goal but that interventions that aim to mobilize communities necessarily adopt different characteristics in different circumstances. Public service announcements may be perceived as contradicting official power and policies.

When access to national media is limited or extremely conditional, grassroots strategies whether community participation and local media could offer an alternative. But if populations are afraid of participating for fear of repression or because of past frustrations, then, participatory approaches face clear obstacles and may not be advisable.

3. *Integration of "top-down" and "bottom-up" approaches:* Faced with different scenarios and choices, the growing consensus is that a multiple approach that combines "top-down" and "bottom-up" interventions is recommended. Here it becomes evident that development communication has gone beyond transmission models focused on implementing behavior changes through communication activities.

The Iringa Nutrition Improvement Program in Tanzania has been mentioned as a successful example of integrating media advocacy, social mobilization and social marketing. The Program included the mobilization of different groups at different levels, community participation, media advocacy to popularize the goals of fighting malnutrition and child mortality, and social marketing to raise awareness among all sectors of the populations. It included "child growth monitoring, strengthening the health infrastructure, health education, and women's activities."

Government commitment, long-term sustainability of the program, and anti-poverty efforts have been mentioned as decisive in contributing to its success in reducing malnutrition despite larger economic problems. Environmental factors such as a tradition of grassroots participation and national policies that dramatically increased literacy were crucial for the success of the program.

4. *Integration of multimedia and interpersonal communication*: Much of the current thinking is that successful interventions combine media channels and interpersonal communication. Against arguments of powerful media effects that dominated development communication in the past, recent conclusions suggest that blending media and interpersonal channels is fundamental for effective interventions.

The media are extremely important in raising awareness and knowledge about a given problem. The media are able to expose large amounts of people to messages and generate conversation among audiences and others who were not exposed. But it would be wrong to assume that development mainly or only requires media channels. Because social learning and decision-making are not limited to considering media messages but listening and exchanging opinions with a number of different sources, interventions cannot solely resort to the mass media.

Although television, radio and other media are important in disseminating messages, social networks are responsible for the diffusion of new ideas. Entertainment-education programming is one way, for example to activate social networks and peer communication in the diffusion of information. Similarly, information given through the media is also important in raising awareness and knowledge as integrated into peer conversations and in contacts with field workers.

According to McKee, interpersonal communication and the actions of community workers account for much of the success of several projects. Nothing can replace community involvement and education in the effective dissemination of information.

Media-centered models are insufficient for behavior change. McKee argues that the most successful strategies in family planning, HIV/AIDS, nutritional and diarrhea programs have involved multiple channels, including strong, community-based programming, networks, peer counseling and government and NGO field workers. Successful initiatives attest to the fact that redundancy and multiple channels should be used.

The media has powerful effects only indirectly by stimulating peer communication and thus making possible for messages to enter social networks and become part of everyday interactions. Without disputing the value of interpersonal communication, McDivitt, Zimick and Hornik have stressed the importance of the mass media in behavior change. In an evaluation of the impact of a vaccination campaign in the Philippines, they concluded that the media, rather than interpersonal channels, was responsible for changes in vaccination knowledge.

Media exposure was sufficient to generate more knowledge about the specifics of the campaign and change in vaccinations without the intervention of social networks. It would be wrong, according to the researchers, to ignore the unmatched reach of the media, particularly among certain groups, in getting the message out. Mass media messages per se, however, do not explain the success of the campaign. The campaign provided specific information that mothers needed in order to engage in expected behaviors, and other conditions (access to health centers, sufficient vaccine supplies) were also fundamental in making behavior change possible.

5. *Personal and environmental approaches should be integrated*: The revision of traditional health promotion strategies and then integration of social marketing and

social mobilization are examples of the tendency to integrate personal and environmental approaches. Consider the "ecological approach" as an example in that direction as used in the North Karelia Project in Finland, the Minnesota Health program, and the Stanford Three Community study. It espouses organizational and environmental interventions and aims to be more comprehensive that efforts directed only at individuals or social action.

Nonbehavioral factors such as unemployment, poverty, and lack of education are included as part of the broad view that ecological approaches encompass. Health promotion should be integrated into existing social systems such as schools, health delivery systems and community organizations. The mentioned projects required coordination among a variety of intermediate agencies that acted as liaisons between developers of health promotion innovation and potential adopters. The focus is still on behavior change but programs feature environmental supports to encourage individuals to adopt and maintain changes.

Similarly, community participation approaches have recognized the need to promote a "holistic approach" that integrates the contributions of both personal behavior change and broader environmental changes in facilitating health improvement.

"Communication for social change" (CSC) is another example of recent efforts to integrate different theories and approaches in development communication. Whereas traditional interventions were based on behavior-change models, CSC relies on participatory approaches in emphasizing the notion of dialogue as central to development. Development is conceived as involving work to "improve the lives of the politically and economically marginalized".

In contrast to the sender-receiver, information-based premises of the dominant paradigm, it stresses the importance of horizontal communication, the role of people as agents of change, and the need for negotiating skills and partnership. Another important contribution of CSC is to call attention to the larger communication environment surrounding populations. In contrast to behavior change and participatory theories that, for different reasons, pay little if any attention to the wide organization of information and media resources, CSC calls attention to the relevance of ongoing policy and structural changes in providing new opportunities for communication interventions.

Unlike neo-dependency theories that negatively view worldwide changes in media and information industries as stimulating a process of power concentration, CSC offers a mixed evaluation. It recognizes that transformations open possibilities for community-based, decentralized forms of participation, but also admits that some characteristics of contemporary media are worrisome in terms of the potential for social change. CSC views changes in health and in quality of life in general in terms of citizens' empowerment, a notion that became more relevant in behavior change models. But unlike participatory theories, CSC stresses the need to define precise indicators to measure the impact of interventions. It is particularly sensitive to the expectations of funding agencies to find results of interventions, and to the needs of communities to provide feedback and actively intervene in projects. Here accountability, a concept that is also fundamental in contemporary global democratic projects, is crucial to development efforts.

Projects should be accountable to participants in order to improve and change interventions and involve those who are ultimately the intended protagonists and beneficiaries. Because the intended goals are somewhat different from behavior-change approaches, then, it is necessary to develop a different set of indicators that tell us whether changes are achieved (although certainly some measurements traditionally used in health interventions are useful too).

The goals are not only formulated in terms that could perfectly fit health promotion/social marketing/behavior change theories (e.g. elimination of HIV/AIDS, lower child and maternal mortality) but also in broader social terms such as eradicating poverty and violence, and increasing employment and gender equality. These goals express a more comprehensive understanding of development that is not limited to "better health and well-being" but is aware of the need to place traditional approaches in larger social and environmental contexts.

Despite the cross-pollination of traditions and a multi-strategy approach to interventions, the rift between behavior change and participatory approaches and theories still characterizes the field. For participatory and advocacy approaches, behavior change models are still associated with a certain scientific paradigm that is questionable on several grounds. Behavior change models are based on premises that do not necessarily translate to developing countries. From a perspective influenced by recent theoretical developments in the social sciences, particularly post-colonial and post-modernist thinking, critics have challenged Western models of rationality and knowledge that inform behavior models.

What is necessary is to change the traditional perspective according to which "traditional cultures" are backward and antithetical to development interventions. Because what populations know is considered wrong, local knowledge is viewed as obstacle and unnecessary in development interventions. Overcoming ethnocentric conceptions is crucial. It requires to recognize that understandings of information and knowledge are different. Interventions also need to be sensitive to the fact that local cultures do not necessarily fit philosophical assumptions about individual rationality that are embedded in traditional models.

Sense-making practices that are found in the developing world contradict key premises of behavior change models. Behavior models assume that individuals engage in certain actions after weighing costs and benefits of the action. Whereas individual interest and achievement are the underlying premises of those models, non-rationalistic forms of knowledge as well community values are central to non-Western cultures.

Critics charge behavior change models for being focused on individual changes while underplaying the need to instrument larger political transformations that affect the quality of life. They call attention to the organizational structures that inhibit the successful implementation of projects for social change.

The concentration of information resources worldwide, the growing power of advertising in media systems, and the intensification of inequalities that underlie the persistence of development problems require more than ever to examine structural-political factors. Media systems have changed dramatically in the last decades. These changes, however, have been particularly revolutionary in the non-Western world as privatization and liberalization of media systems radically transformed the production, distribution, and availability of information resources.

Behavior change models have recognized the merits of insights from participatory approaches as well as the need to be sensitive to media access and new technologies. They continue to be mainly concerned with refining analytical and evaluation instruments and measuring the success of different intervention strategies. One of the main tasks is to identify the impact of communication/ information campaigns in the context of other factors that affect behavior. The integration of social mobilization and social marketing strategies has been found to be successful and a positive referent for future interventions.

Emerging Trends in Communciation Development

Although communication technologies have dominated the discourse around recent developments in information and communications, there have been equally rapid and fundamental changes in the wider communication environment in which most communication initiatives operate, particularly regarding new technologies and the media. There are perhaps seven key trends, some of them contradictory, which have emerged over the last decade and particularly over the last five years:

New technologies, principally in the form of the internet as well as mobile telecommunications, are creating major new opportunities for disseminating information, networking, amplifying marginalised voices and for creating synergies between new and old media. The potential of allying the pow er of the internet with the reach of radio offers particularly strong opportunities to create more knowledge based societies. New technologies are creating much more information based, increasingly horizontally networked and highly complex communications environments. They are leading to increasing information saturation for those who are connected, but also potentially major new forms of information (and therefore political and economic) exclusion for those who are not.

Media liberalisation: A major liberalisation and opening up of the media in much of the developing world, particularly Africa, transforming both print and broadcast media from a largely government owned, monopolistic and uncreative media environment to a more dynamic, popular, democratic, creative and complex one. The print media have, despite their sometimes limited readership, played a critical role in providing increased internal scrutiny of governments, and a free press has become increasingly regarded as a precondition for effective and sustainable development and good governance. The number of print titles in many countries has increased rapidly, and while many of these rise and fall rapidly, particularly during election periods, many have been able to sustain themselves both financially and retain a genuine political independence from government.

The broadcast media have also been transformed in many countries, with competition ushering in a new environment of choice and creativity in programming, with many new private and community radio and television stations rapidly establishing audience dominance over old state run broadcasting systems. Private radio stations, while often criticised for relying heavily on formulaic, music based programming, have also been praised for the opportunities they are providing for on-air discussions and for creating important new spaces for genuinely public debate.

This new environment has also created opportunities for the more rapid emergence of a community based media, although new regulatory environments in several countries have proved unsupportive to the development of genuine community media movements. Satellite broadcasting of television, and more recently in digital radio, is adding a further layer to an increasingly complex media environment.

Consumerism: Liberalisation has led not only to greater media freedoms, but also to the emergence of an increasingly consumer led, business oriented, advertising driven and urban centred communication infrastructure, one that is arguably less and less interested in the concerns of the poor, and in the case of broadcast media, decreasingly interested in providing news and information to its audiences.

State run broadcasting systems have found it difficult to transform themselves into public broadcasting entities and are generally in decline, with a concomitant decline in language programming and the lack of strong and relevant programming of most concern to rural people. In the case of print media, journalists are finding it increasingly difficult to secure editorial space and resources to report on issues of most concern to the poor, and particularly to travel to rural areas, and there are in many cases few er and few er journalists who are interested in doing so. This is arguably leading to an increasing "invisibility" of the poor, and poverty related issues, in public and political debate. The print media in many countries are also becoming increasingly "localised" and national in their outlook and editors are reporting less and less interest in international stories, particularly stories from other parts of the developing world.

The advertising driven nature of the media is also leading to highly sexualised, stereotypical images and messages around the role of women in society, images that have long been criticised in the North but are far more pervasive within many developing countries as a result of liberalisation.

Media freedom and freedom of expression: Media freedoms have been hard won and fought for but remain under constant threat in many countries. New international networks have emerged to help protect media freedoms and donors have increasingly made their support conditional on governments guaranteeing free media. New technologies have made censorship and state control of information far more difficult.

While there has been a general global trend tow ards much greater media freedom, sometimes this trend has been confined largely to urban metropolitan middle classes rather than the population as a whole.

Globalisation and transnational ownership of the media is resulting in an increasing concentration of ownership of media and communications organisations internationally, with increasing numbers of mainstream developing country media institutions being bought by trans-national conglomerates. For most Southern based media, reliance on Northern based news sources for international news has grown rather than diminished and, with the exception of internet based news services, the number of independent southern based news and information sources has decreased, and the degree of regional reporting –and consequently of public understanding of events and attitudes in neighbouring countries – has declined.

Women continue to suffer marginalisation in and from communication networks, and evidence of the scale of sexual harassment and discrimination within the media itself in Africa is growing. When in 1995, UNESCO sponsored a global media monitoring project to explore the representation of women in 71 countries, it found that women made up just 17 per cent of all interviewees in the news world-wide. Women interviewees were much more likely to be lay voices, even on topics which were very woman-focused. Male interviewees were more typically interview ed as voices of authority. 29% of all female interviewees were portrayed as victims of crime or accidents, compared with just 10% of male interviewees. A follow-up world-wide study in 2000 has found similar results and these are relatively consistent across regions. Similar findings have been repeated in many national studies. A further tw ist in the story is the split in news coverage between urban and rural concerns – the latter receiving comparatively little attention. In one Kenyan study, rural women featured in a tiny fraction of news coverage and a striking 76% of rural women who appeared in the media were portrayed as criminals or victims.

Media and conflict: The media continue to play a critical role in relation to the fuelling, and sometimes in the alleviation, of regional tensions and conflict. Nationalistic, sensational and ill-informed media remains a major problem in some countries, and is making a major contribution to inciting public resentment, hatred and intolerance to neighbouring countries, migrant communities or particular minorities.

Emergence of Knowledge Societies

Debates and focus on the potential of communication technologies, combined with a grow ing understanding and acknowledgement of the role of information and "knowledge" in development, have helped to transform donor and international agency attitudes to the role of information in development. Five years ago, the role of communication and information in alleviating poverty, promoting equity and achieving sustainable development remained in the same position as it had for many years: on the margins of development agendas.

Today, the role of information, knowledge, communication and advocacy in development is better recognised and arguably has a higher profile than ever before. While these areas continue to be chronically underresourced and continue to face major evaluation challenges in terms of demonstrating impact and sustainability, they have moved emphatically from the periphery to the mainstream of donor agendas. There are many reasons for this shift, with governments increasingly recognising the development implications of transational information flows, or the concerns over the "digital divide", the potential of new communication technologies, and the grow ing characterisation of humanity living increasingly in global information societies driven by global knowledge economies. Perhaps the key events and trends have been:

In December 1998, the World Bank focused its keynote World Development Report on *Knowledge for Development*. In doing so, the Bank was signalling its own intended transformation from being principally an economic entity into becoming a "knowledge bank", where the expertise and accumulated wisdom that it held and could access was becoming as important as the money it could lend and dispense.

The report sparked substantial debate both within the development community and within the Bank itself, with many welcoming the shift as a further sign of the evolution of the Bank's thinking away from a "postWashington consensus" view of economics to one which was more socially oriented. Others criticised the Bank for its apparent view that the principal problem facing developing countries was one of ignorance, combined with fears in conflating the terms "information" and "knowledge", that the report apparently did not address the problem of who judges what is and is not knowledge. The centrepiece of the Bank's "knowledge bank strategy was the development of a new *Global Development Gateway*, a highly controversial internet initiative designed to bring together on one supersite all the available "knowledge" on development issues. The initiative met with criticism from civil society organisations who argued (and continue to argue) that it represented an unnecessary duplication and competition to existing initiatives, that editorial control of the site is too heavily centralised within the Bank itself or within participating governments, that while consultation processes around the Gateway have been significant, very little change has resulted from them, that the Gateway, in attempting to centralise information in one place, ignores the fundamental advantage of the internet in enabling a highly decentralised architecture in information recovery; and that the exercise is an unjustifiably expensive use of Bank funds. The Gateway how ever has been developed and still plans to be the largest portal for development information in the world.

The Bank also went on, among several other initiatives, to support the Global Knowledge Partnership, a major grouping of donors, governments, international organisations and some civil society organisations which organised a major Global Knowledge II conference in Kuala Lumpur in 2000. That conference mapped out a "Global Knowledge Action Plan" which committed key participants to supporting a range of initiatives under the general titles of Facilitating knowledge exchange and content creation; Building networks and partnerships; Addressing policy and regulatory frameworks; Promoting advocacy, empowerment and governance; and Promoting community based social development.

The debate on knowledge was inextricably linked, and largely driven by, the increasing recognition of the potential of communication technologies in development. While some organisations closely connected to Communication for Development Roundtable meetings, such as IDRC, have been pioneering and advocating the use of ICTs for many years, it is only in the last half decade that they have so radically begun to inform development strategies and agendas. A series of major conferences, policy initiatives, and international reports have contributed to this change. It is impossible to list here all the hundreds of events that have occurred over the last two or three years in this area although two recent developments are perhaps worth highlighting here.

One is the Human Development Report 2001, *Making technologies work for human development*, a bold and highly optimistic report arguing that both information and genetic technologies offer huge promise in tackling fundamental poverty "*Often those* with the least have least to fear from the future" and it put forw ard six main arguments.

1. The technology divide does not have to follow the income divide, and throughout history, technology has

been a pow erful tool for human development and poverty reduction.

2. The market is a pow erful tool of technological progress, but it is not pow erful enough to create and diffuse the technologies needed to eradicate poverty.
3. Developing countries may gain especially high rew ards from new technologies, but they also face especially severe challenges in managing the risks.
4. The technology revolution and globalization are creating a network age, and that is changing how technology is created and diffused.
5. Even in the network age, domestic policy still matters. All countries, even the poorest, need to implement policies that encourage innovation, access and the development of advanced skills.
6. National policies will not be sufficient to compensate for global market failures.

Rules and Regulations to Channel New Technologies

New international initiatives and the fair use of global rules are needed to channel new technologies tow ards the most urgent needs of the world's poor people. In 2000, the G8 countries at their Okinaw a meeting made the issue of communication technologies a major theme of their summit. The summit, which was held on an island inaccessible to protesters, drew criticism from many civil society organisations for failing to take significant action on developing country debt relief (thus prompting the burning of laptop computers in protest). The summit did nevertheless follow through on its commitment to set up a Digital Opportunities Task (DOT) Force.

The DOT Force was a highly unusual initiative for the G8, with task forces constituting in each G8 country of a representative each from government, industry and civil society, with additional representatives from a small number of developing countries. The report of the DOT Force was finalised in mid 2001 and presented and approved at its Genoa meeting, although the issues it dealt with were overshadow ed by the focus on the violence surrounding the meeting, and the focus on anti globalisation protests. The DOT Force made 9 key recommendations which it committed itself to implementing:

— *Action Point 1*: Help establish and support developing country and emerging economy strategies

— *Action Point 2*: Improve connectivity, increase access and low er costs

— *Action Point 3*: Enhance human capacity development, knowledge creation and sharing

— *Action Point 4*: Foster enterprise and entrepreneurship for sustainable economic development

— *Action Point 5*: Establish and support universal participation in addressing new international policy and technical issues raised by the internet and

— *Action Point 6:* Establish and support dedicated initiatives for the ICT inclusion of the least developed countries

— *Action Point 7:* Promote ICT for health care and in support against HIV/AIDS and other infectious and communicable diseases

— *Action Point 8:* National and international effort to support local content and applications creation

— *Action Point 9*: Prioritise ICT in G8 and other development assistance policies and programmes and enhance coordination of multilateral initiatives.

A new ICT Task Force has just been launched and is mandated by UN Secretary-General Kofi Annan to find new, creative and quick-acting means to spread the benefits of the digital revolution from which four billion of the world's people are currently excluded. The members of the Task Force come from the public and private sectors, from civil society and the scientific community, and from leaders of the developing as well as the most technologically advanced countries.

Task Force priorities, below, are defined by the ECOSOC 2000 Ministerial Declaration.

1. To forge strategic partnerships between the United Nations system, private industry, trusts and foundations, donor governments, programme countries, and other relevant international actors.
2. To pool the experiences of both developed and developing countries in introducing and promoting ICT for development.
3. To develop innovative modalities for strengthening the ICT capacity of the developing countries.
4. To assist Member States in creation of national ICT strategies, policy frameworks, and regulatory environment to ensure connectivity and universal access to ICT.
5. To promote ICT for development applications: building human resources and institutional capacity, including e-health, e-education, e-government, and ecommerce.

6. To mobilise new and additional resources - financial, technical, and human - for promoting and funding ICT-for-development programmes and projects.

While many donors and international agencies are fundamentally reviewing their approach to communication technologies, for some this is also leading to a more fundamental thinking on the role of information in development per se. The ICT debate is combining with debates on a wider set of issues, such as knowledge, good governance, global inclusion and a greater focus on development strategies being owned by developing country societies, to create increasing institutional debates and renew ed interest in the role of information in development.

Another major, and accelerating, development over recent years is the emergence of a global civil society. While increasingly strong and dynamic civil societies at a national level have been developing and been recognised for several years, the scale and impact of a global civil society, principally enabled by ease of communication through email and the web, is a more recently recognised phenomenon. The publication of an inaugural Global Civil Society Yearbook in 2001 by the London School of Economics saw the coming of age of this concept.

It is arguably the women's movement which has been at the forefront of this development, first with the evolution of a formidably organised, coherent and effective caucus around the Beijing and Cairo conferences, and more recently with a series of initiatives carving out international spaces on the internet and using this to take forw ard a global movement.

One example is WomenWatch, a joint UN project to create a core Internet space on global women's issues. It was created to monitor the results of the Fourth World Conference on Women, held in Beijing in 1995. It was founded in March 1997 by the Division for the Advancement of Women (DAW), the United Nations Development Fund for Women (UNIFEM) and the International Research and Training Institute for the Advancement of Women (INSTRAW), together with other UN and other international partners.

One of the most remarkable of the initiatives from Womenw atch was an online email debate set up in preparation for Beijing +5 review. 10,000 individuals joined the debate which covered 12 critical areas of concerns, each area running for 6 weeks. 1,000 people contributed substantively to the debate, the average ratio: 52% from north, 48% from south. The debate generated information on shared and unique obstacles, lessons and practices. Another key development is the emergence of Oneworld.net, a global network of civil society organisations, with a partnership now of more than 1,200 civil society partners grouped around a grow ing network of 10 Oneworld Centres.

Although not explicitly civil society based, another major portal in the field of communications has emerged in the form of the Communication Initiative. A combination of the interest in new technologies, an increasing recognition of the importance of the role of communication in development, and a hunger among communication practitioners worldwide for better information sharing and understanding on communication issues was captured very successfully by the creation of the Communication Initiative. The Initiative is a partnership of major development organisations seeking to support advances in the effectiveness and scale of communication interventions for positive international development. The Initiative has become the key point of reference for debates and news for communication practitioners in this field.

The International Telecommunication Union organised a major two stage "summit", the World Summit on the Information Society, the aim of which was to develop a common vision and understanding of the Information Society and to draw up a strategic plan of action for concerted development towards realizing this vision. The Summit also provided a unique opportunity to gather the world community to assemble at a high level and to develop a better understanding of this revolution and its impact.

Bibliography

Ang, Ien, "Living Room Wars: Rethinking Media Audiences for a Postmodern World", New York: Routledge, 1996.

Baldwin, Thomas, "Convergence: Integrating Media, Information, and Communication", Thousand Oaks: Sage Publications, 1996.

Banket, V. L., and V. M. Dorofeev, *Digital Methods in Satellite Communications,* Moscow: Radio & Svyaz, 1988.

Bar, Francois, et al. 1999, "Defending the Internet Revolution in the Broadband Era: When Doing Nothing Is Doing Harm," August, 1999.

Beniger, James, *The Control Revolution: Technological and Economic Origins of the Information Society*, Harvard University Press, Cambridge, Mass.: 1986.

Beierle, Thomas, and Sarah Cahill Electronic Democracy and Environmental Governance: A Survey of the States, Resources for the Future, *Discussion Paper 00-42,* October 2000, 30 p.

Bennahum, David S, "The Myth of Digital Nirvana." *Educomm Review 31.5* (September/October 1996).

Berkowe, Kathleen Hawkins, 2000, "Open Access to Cable Systems for Internet Access Providers", Media Law and Policy VIII (2).

Beierle, Thomas, and Sarah Cahill Electronic Democracy and Environmental Governance: A Survey of the States, Resources for the Future, *Discussion Paper 00-42,* October 2000, 30 p.

Bennahum, David S., "The Myth of Digital Nirvana." *Educomm Review 31.5* (September/October 1996).

Center for Democracy and Technology (CDT), 2000, Broadband Backgrounder: Public Policy Issues Raised by Broadband Technology, Washington, D.C.: CDT, December.

Center for Media Education (CME), 2001, "Broadband Networks and Narrow Visions: The Internet at Risk." Washington, D.C.: CME.

Centerwall, B.S., "Exposure to television as a cause of violence," in Comstock G., (ed) *Public Communications as Behavior*, Orlando, FL: Academic Press, Inc., 1989.

Mander, Jerry, *Four Arguments for the Elimination of Television*, New York: Morrow, 1977.

Index

Canadian International Development Agency (CIDA) 210
Civic sector conversations 93
Civil society organizations 103
Commercial cable network 93
Communication for Social Change (CSC) 123, 206, 275
Communication Initiative Latin America (CILA) 209
Communication strategies 7
Communications infrastructures 96
Communications technologies 96
Community participation 3
Community-based organizations 100
Consumerism 281
Cross-fertilization 134

Development Support Communication 219
Digital Opportunities Task (DOT) 287
Dynamic communications environments 101

Economic liberalization 101
Entertainment Education (EE) 207, 235

Globalisation 282
Gulf Cooperation Council (GCC) 136

Horizontal communication 109
Human communication theories 235
Human-centered approach 248

Immemorial phenomeniological responsibility 93
Immunization programs 226
Information Communication Technologies (ICT's) 104, 213
International framework of intellectual property rights 128
International Telecommunication Union 292
Interpersonal communication 238
Interpersonal conflict 200

Marginalisation 6
Marketing research techniques 229
Media advocacy theory 258
Media-centered perspective 96
Media-centered persuasion activities 218
Media-centrism 220

Modernization theory 216

Non-governmental organisations 7

Nonprofit organizations 223

Participatory communication 211

Participatory theories 243

People-to-people communication 106

Political liberalization 101

Program-centered funding 94

Social change communities 94

Social marketing
- approach 222
- interventions 227
- theory 223

South Asian Partnership Canada (SAP) 210

Strategic communications 88

Technological determinism 96

Telecommunications 106

Top-down approach 244

Traditional communication strategies 213

Traditional social marketing approaches 262

Transformative communities 94

UN General Assembly Special Session (UNGASS) 117

United Nations Development Fund for Women (UNIFEM) 291

United Nations Educational, Scientific and Cultural Organisation (UNESCO) 219

United Nations International Children's Emergency 260

World Health Organization 233